Non-recourse loans are a unique way to leverage your IRA and bring in more income from larger properties. North American Savings Bank is able to guide you through this money making process. Grasp it, and you can make up for lost time in retirement earnings.

–Adriane Berg, author of
"How Not To Go Broke At 102: Achieving Everlasting Wealth"

North American Savings Bank envisioned the use of non-recourse lending within certain self-directed IRAs and took the lead in establishing a comprehensive program to educate and assist individual investors seeking to further diversify their retirement investment portfolios with the addition of alternative assets, such as real estate. Millennium Trust believes there is great value in helping educate investors on every aspect of real estate investing within self-directed individual retirement accounts.

–Sandra Reese, SVP Real Estate Investing,
Millennium Trust Company

When our clients need an IRA lender to make their real estate transactions happen, we readily provide NASB's name with confidence. As an IRA-focused lender, NASB understands the unique needs and structure required and has the experience and people to deliver its services quickly and professionally.

–Jeffrey A. Kelley, Chief Operating Officer, Sterling Trust Company

Investors who want to use leverage to buy real estate in their IRAs need to understand that the IRS requires that they use a non-recourse loan, and it is important that they work with a lender that can explain to the investor the unique requirements of those loans so that they know exactly what to expect and do what they can to protect their investment. Being a lender that understands non-recourse loans has made NASB a valuable resource for our clients.

–Tom Gonnella, Vice President,
Lincoln Trust Company (formerly Fiserv Investment Support Services)

In 2001–2002, individuals across the nation suffered devastating losses to the traditional investments within their retirement accounts. During this same time frame, real estate was growing at a rapid pace and created a very attractive opportunity for investing retirement funds. One missing component was a lending institution that would provide the required non-recourse loans to take advantage of the opportunity.

North American Savings Bank stepped up and became the leading source of non-recourse loan programs specifically designed to address the needs of self-directed IRAs on a national basis. To this day, they are the premier non-recourse loan provider in the self-directed IRA industry, known for a quality loan product at reasonable pricing. Their programs allow individuals to take control over their retirement investment future. My compliments and whole-hearted thanks to Matt Allen and his team of professionals for taking a significant step forward into what was then uncharted territory.

**–Michael P. Scott, VP, Director of Business Development,
PENSCO Trust Company**

For many years clients at Equity Trust have successfully worked with both Matt Allen and North American Savings Bank to utilize non-recourse loans for real estate investments in their retirement accounts.

Currently, many Americans are looking for financial security in their retirement accounts through diversification. The concept of utilizing non-recourse loan for real estate investments can be very effective for financial security and wealth creation.

This book goes a long way in demystifying the process and I would like to congratulate Matt on a job well done.

**–Richard A. Desich, Co-Founder of Equity Trust Company
and former president of the Retirement Industry Trust Association (RITA)**

NASB was the pioneer that first brought non-recourse lending for IRAs to a national audience. Their experience encompasses working with clients from a diversity of custodians, administrators, and facilitators. This gives them a unique perspective on how to harness the power of leverage inside a self-directed IRA.

–Jeremy Ames, President and Cofounder, Guidant Financial Group, Inc.

I've had the privilege of working with Matt and NASB for the past six to seven years and know they deliver a highly personalized level of service and industry-leading knowledge for clients seeking lending for their IRA real estate transactions. Count on Matt and NASB to go above and beyond expectations both in delivery of exceptional service and their innovative approach to business.

–Kelli Click, VP, Business Development and Marketing, Self-Directed IRA Services, Inc.

At Sunwest Trust, Inc., we specialize in acting as custodian for nontraditional asset IRAs, and I believe real estate is one of the best. If you are a seasoned real estate investor, you already know how leverage can really increase your yield on real estate, and NASB is one of the only banks in the country that can and does provide the kind of financing you must have inside an IRA. NASB understands the special requirements of dealing with an IRA and they understand real estate.

–Terry White, CEO, Sunwest Trust, Inc.

As a CPA, tax specialist, and host of KMBZ's Moneyline program, I have been amazed by how little the American public, brokers, and investment advisors know about IRAs and retirement accounts. IRAs can be used to buy or start up a business and IRAs, and many retirement accounts can be used to buy rental properties and other investment real estate—so why not be smart and make 100% use of your money instead of using your after-tax dollars, sometimes as little as 60 or 70% of the cash to buy real estate? Best of all, you can partner with almost anyone and obtain non-recourse loans from the best-known lender, North American Savings Bank. I am always surprised by the number of financial advisors who tell their clients they cannot use their retirement accounts to purchase investment properties. When you get that response, simply go to iralending.com. Get the facts and discover what Americans who don't want the volatility of the markets do: they invest in real estate.

**–Peter Newman, Radio Host of Moneyline
and Owner of Peter Newman, CPA**

In today's economy, it's more important than ever to find a bank you can trust and North American Savings Bank stands out for many reasons—they're extremely knowledgeable, personalized, and transparent. Whether you're seeking a non-recourse loan for your IRA or a traditional mortgage, NASB listens to their customers and gets results quickly. As their marketing consultant, I know personally they are responsive and dedicated to their customers.

–Robyn Levin, Founder/CEO, R. Levin Marketing Group

NASB has enabled several clients of Security Trust Company to make real estate purchases with their self-directed IRA. In fact, one Security Trust client was able to buy a $448,000 property with just $166,000 in cash from her IRA. Investments such as this could not have been made without NASB and the use of their non-recourse loan product, which allows STC's clients to leverage their IRAs and invest in larger properties in today's exciting real estate market.

–John Laughlin, President, Security Trust Company

NASB has been a pleasure to deal with and understands the IRA non-recourse market.

–Steven D. Rothberg, Esq., Executive Vice President, The Capital Companies

NASB has been, and continues to be, the leader in non-recourse loans to qualified accounts. Many of our IRA participants have funded loans with NASB and all have had a very pleasant experience. Historically, there has been reluctance, on the part of retirement plan participants, to leverage their real estate investments. I believe the information in this book will help eliminate their concerns by providing valuable information regarding the loan process, the tax considerations and the financial benefits. I am fortunate to be acquainted with, Matt, Eric and Tom, all of whom are extremely knowledgeable professionals.

–Michael McNair, Vice President & Trust Officer, IRA Services Trust Company

Truly self-directed IRAs provide the public with a wide range of investment options over and above those available through plans offered by Investment Product Sponsors. This benefits the users (plan participants) by giving them the ability to diversify their investment choices within the plan at any time, hopefully therefore reducing the risk to their retirement portfolios.

–James Wagner, Self-directed IRA industry expert

According to **MSN MONEY***, "Most investors believe they cannot use IRA money to buy real estate, developed or undeveloped ... but, they are wrong." The fact is that by utilizing a real estate IRA, an investor can purchase income-producing real estate to hold within their portfolio. Not only that, but this form of self-directed IRA can also obtain mortgage financing. The leader in the field of IRA mortgage lending is NASB ... hands down.*

–Robert Hubbard, Founder and CEO, Safeguard Financial

When our clients are interested in purchasing real property with debt financing, we refer them to North American Savings Bank. The people at NASB are always responsive and informative.

–Pamela Constantino, President, Polycomp Trust Company

NASB has been a great resource for our clients. In an economic climate where clients are looking for alternative investment options, NASB has led the industry in providing banking solutions that fit a client's unique needs.

–Theresa A. Fette, Chief Operating Officer, Provident Trust Group

Every investor of every size has an immediate need to diversify their investment portfolio. Portfolio diversification is the key to a stable, reliable, and consistent return on your investments. The ability to purchase real estate inside of your IRA is a fundamental step into a truly diversified investment portfolio. My career as a community banker has proven overwhelmingly how important leverage is to producing the highest return on your investment. Non-recourse lending is an effective way for the investor to insure their success.

–Doug Lawson, President/CEO,
My Retirement Account Services, LLC (MyRA)

Asset Exchange Strategies, LLC works closely with leading funding institutions such as North American Savings Bank to help investors structure an investment that is compliant with IRS regulations. North American Savings Bank has provided many of our clients with expedient funding services which has resulted in a profitable gain in their retirement account.

–Daniel Cordoba, CEO, Asset Exchange Strategies, LLC and author of
"From Wall Street to Main Street, Your Guide to Self-Directed Investing"

LEVERAGE
YOUR IRA

Maximize Your Profits with
REAL ESTATE

LEVERAGE
YOUR IRA

Maximize Your Profits with
REAL ESTATE

MATTHEW M. ALLEN

with Eric Wikstrom, CPA, CFP®,
Tom W. Anderson, and Edwin Kelly

LIFESUCCESS PUBLISHING, LLC
8900 E Pinnacle Peak Road, Suite D240
Scottsdale, AZ, 85255

Telephone:	800.473.7134
Fax:	480.661.1014
E-mail:	admin@lifesuccesspublishing.com
ISBN:	978-1-59930-097-9

Cover:	LifeSuccess Publishing, LLC
Text:	Lloyd Arbour, LifeSuccess Publishing, LLC

Edit:	Publication Services

COMPANIES, ORGANIZATIONS, INSTITUTIONS, AND INDUSTRY PUBLICATIONS. Quantity discounts are available on bulk purchases of this book for reselling, educational purposes, subscription incentives, gifts, sponsorship, or fundraising. Special books or book excerpts can also be created to fit specific needs such as private labeling with your logo on the cover and a message from a VIP printed inside. For more information, please contact our Special Sales Department at LifeSuccess Publishing, LLC.

This work is not intended and should not be relied upon, as a professional opinion or advice on any legal, tax or investment aspects of IRAs. IRA owners considering an IRA investment in real property should consult with their own legal, tax and investment advisor(s). The list of custodians/administrators/companies in this book is not exhaustive. An entity's identification or exclusion in this book is not in any way an endorsement, referral, judgment, opinion or analysis as to any firm's level of expertise or financial condition.

The information in this book is for educational purposes only and is not to be construed as investment advise. The authors and publishers are not responsible for any losses incurred using any of the strategies discussed in this book. Please consult with an investment adviser or tax adviser to ensure these types of investments are suitable for your situation.

IRA Lending™ and America's IRA Non-Recourse Lender™ are trademarks owned exclusively by North American Savings Bank.

FOREWORD

by Bruce Thielen

North American Savings Bank first offered its IRA Non-Recourse Loan product in 2004 when we were approached by one of our banking customers for this specific type of loan. Our customer was having difficulty finding a lender who would provide financing for the purchase of rental properties within a self-directed IRA. He was told he could not obtain financing because the property would be owned by his self-directed IRA rather than in his name as an individual. The borrower was purchasing 2 duplex investment properties and wanted to borrow 50% of the purchase price. My first thought was, we have to find a way to make these loans for our customer. This loan seemed like a perfect fit for our loan portfolio. NASB has been a portfolio lender since 1927 with more than 20 years of experience offering non-conforming loans to borrowers who do not fit the secondary market guidelines. NASB is one of the top Internet mortgage lenders in the United States, serving all 50 States and the District of Columbia.

Our customer was working with a self-directed IRA custodian to manage his IRA accounts. I had several conversations with this custodian to figure out how best to structure our customer's transaction while maintaining IRS compliance and to assist in my own comfort level with the process. After working out the legal details with the custodian, the title vendor and our attorney, I concluded that we not only could finance this purchase, but we might help other IRA investors to leverage their IRA holdings to purchase real estate. I was encouraged to consider offering an IRA loan program nationwide since there were no lenders offering this product. In 2005, we formally launched our IRA loan program and website www. iralending.com. Since that time we've been the nationwide leader in non-recourse lending to self-directed retirement plans such as IRAs, solo (k) plans and IRA LLCs.

Over the past 5+ years, we have closed over $150 million in IRA loans representing more than 1,000 transactions across the United States. Investing in real estate can be a good way for many IRA investors to diversify their retirement portfolio, especially if you have experience with real estate investments. We also understand that using IRA funds to invest in real estate is not for everyone. We certainly do not recommend that an investor invest all of their IRA assets into a single investment property or investment vehicle. However, the recent downturn in the real estate market is presenting exceptional opportunities for smart real estate investors who can purchase foreclosed or distressed real estate at substantial market discounts. Using your IRA to invest in real estate can provide stable returns for years to come while building real equity.

You will find many resources in this book to fully educate you about the process of investing your retirement funds in real estate. These chapters are written by the nation's experts on self-directed IRAs, accounting and financing real estate within your self-directed IRA. I hope you find this book helpful in learning about the benefits and risks associated with real estate investments for your self-directed retirement plans.

–Bruce Thielen
Senior Vice President
North American Savings Bank

CONTENTS

INTRODUCTION

In recent times, we have all witnessed a new realization that investments can be fickle. Stocks and the broader financial markets have shown significant declines, causing many people to move money from those investments to cash, hoping a better opportunity to enhance their retirement nest eggs will appear. Now it has. Along with the financial decline, real estate prices have readjusted in many areas of the country, offering great deals to investors who understand that real estate is one of the best investments available.

Some investors remember a similar scenario in the 1980s as real estate prices readjusted and then set upon an unprecedented march upward in value over the next 25 years. We are once again perched upon a dawn for those who can recognize the pattern of opportunity.

Many Americans have saved their hard-earned money in tax-advantaged individual retirement accounts (IRAs) and are frustrated because they assume that this money can't be used to take advantage of the windfall in real estate, but this is a false assumption. IRA funds *can* be used to purchase real estate for investment purposes, offering the opportunity to take advantage of both capital appreciation and immediate cash flow into your IRA.

Throughout the pages of this book, we will show you the precise steps involved to master this type of investment and returns that simply can't be found in other areas during our current economic climate. We'll start with a basic introduction to the ideas that motivate each of us when investing our retirement money. This includes the wealth of misinformation offered by financial companies who campaign hard to ensure you only buy their products. This misinformation keeps many people from maximizing their opportunities, and we will dispel any rumors from financial propaganda that could be holding you back.

We'll also discuss the basics of IRAs, how they came to be, and Internal Revenue Service rules governing them. The IRS can seem intimidating to many people, but it need not be. Once you achieve your own comfort level and know for yourself what the rules are, or aren't, you will feel confident that this investment is for you.

For most people, IRAs are just one component of their overall financial plan. By focusing on what you want to achieve for your retirement, you can create a financial plan that helps you meet those goals. Many people who created a financial plan even as recently as five years ago will now find it obsolete given the turbulent market and falling returns in almost every investment class. Real estate can fill that gap, so an updated financial plan is in order to be sure you are still on track for the retirement you want and deserve.

One of the creative products that makes investing IRA funds in real estate a possibility for almost everyone is the advent of the IRA non-recourse loan. This type of financing was created specifically to allow investors the opportunity to use these tax-advantaged retirement funds to build a real estate investment portfolio. We'll explain in detail how it works and why using this type of leverage will allow you maximum gain for minimal money.

This book is a great resource for those who are currently unfamiliar with any kind of real estate investing as well as experienced real estate investors. We discuss the basics of locating and evaluating properties and how to make good decisions about the type and cost of particular types of real estate investments. This includes helpful hints and secrets known to the most experienced real estate investors.

The legal and taxation issues are important to understand—even though you will usually have a qualified professional handling these areas. We have expert Eric Wikstrom, CPA, CFP®, who will explain in detail what you need to know before pursuing this investment strategy and any potential pitfalls that you need to understand.

What happens when you want to sell the real estate owned by your IRA? We have expert Edwin Kelly, Director of Retirement Education Group, an affiliate of Equity Trust Company, to discuss different exit strategies to maximize your returns and reduce the amount of taxes paid (if any) by your retirement plan.

There are certain transactions that are prohibited when using IRA funds. We also have Tom Anderson, Vice Chairman and founder of PENSCO Trust Company, to offer his vast knowledge in the area of prohibited transactions. Tom has outlined an exhaustive list of things you can and cannot do within in your IRA, and he provides a quiz to test your knowledge.

I have also added a frequently asked questions section for those areas that are of most common concern for people. This allows you to simply scan through and get your questions answered quickly and easily.

There are options available that not only allow you the opportunity to gain higher returns, but also to create long-term income through real estate investments.

MEET THE EXPERTS

Matt Allen

Matt Allen is a nationally recognized speaker and author on the subject of IRA non-recourse loans. He makes frequent appearances on radio shows such as *Moneyline* with Peter Newman and contributes regularly to national publications on the subject of self-directed IRAs and non-recourse loans. Matt is a graduate of the University of Missouri and a member of the Retirement Industry Trust Association (RITA).

Matt is the Director of IRA Lending at North American Savings Bank, FSB, a publicly traded company on NASDAQ under the symbol NASB. The company has more than $1.5 billion in assets and has been based in Kansas City, Missouri, since 1927. A leader in the mortgage industry, NASB is a nationwide lender serving all 50 states. NASB provides more than $1 billion in mortgages per year for home purchases, mortgage refinancing, and real estate investment. NASB has remained on the cutting edge by developing products that allow investors to maximize gains within their self-directed IRAs through investment real estate.

Matt has been instrumental in launching the first nationwide non-recourse loan program for self-directed IRAs and teaches investors how to compound their retirement money while diversifying into real estate. Recognized as the expert on self-directed IRA non-recourse loans, Matt focuses on building diversified wealth.

Matt can be reached at:

North American Savings Bank
10950 El Monte, Suite 210
Overland Park, KS 66211
1-866-735-6272 toll free
mallen@nasb.com
www.iralending.com

Eric Wikstrom, CPA, CFP®

Eric Wikstrom has over 25 years of tax, accounting, and corporate finance experience. In 2005, Eric founded Integrated Wealth Strategies, LLC, to help individuals with financial planning and retirement-plan structuring. By educating clients about what the law permits retirement accounts to hold as investments, the client receives a more comprehensive approach to asset allocation than those offered by traditional financial services firms.

Eric has appeared on nationally syndicated radio programs, is a frequent speaker at self-directed IRA educational events and is a technical contributor to the real estate analysis software program "The Landlord's Cash Flow Analyzer." Mr. Wikstrom has contributed to articles in *U.S. News & World Report*, MarketWatch.com and *Ed Slott's IRA Advisor Newsletter*. Eric has also developed an educational training series on self-directed investing for the nation's largest real estate brokerage.

Eric has recently been the featured speaker for the Boston Estate Planning Council, the San Jose Real Estate Investor's Association and the San Francisco Bay Real Estate Expo. Mr. Wikstrom is considered one of the nation's leading experts and speaks frequently on the tax effects on IRAs of the Unrelated Business Income Tax. Eric is a member of the Retirement Industry Trust Association (RITA).

Mr. Wikstrom is a Certified Public Accountant and a Certified Financial Planner who holds securities and life insurance licenses. Eric graduated from the University of Washington with a BA in Business Administration and holds a Master's of Science in Taxation from Golden Gate University in San Francisco, California.

Eric can be reached at:

Integrated Wealth Strategies, LLC
7683 S.E. 27th St., #305
Mercer Island, WA 98040
1-206-949-8236 Direct
ewikstrom@iwealthstrategies.com
www.iwealthstrategies.com

Tom Anderson

Tom Anderson is the Vice Chairman, and founder of PENSCO Trust Company and PENSCO, Inc. He is considered by many to be the national expert, author, and speaker on the topic of self-directed IRAs and plans. In addition, Mr. Anderson focuses on how investors can increase their wealth-building potential with real estate, private equity, and other alternative investments in their retirement accounts. He has contributed articles to the *Wall Street Journal*, the *New York Times*, Bankrate. com, MarketWatch.com, *Fortune*, *Time*, *Forbes*, *Entrepreneur*, *Smart Money*, *Kiplinger's*, and many other publications; has hosted his own radio show; created educational materials for the AICPA; and has appeared on CNBC's *Power Lunch* television show. Mr. Anderson was invited to Washington as part of the Future of Finance Initiative to assist the Obama administration with developing the future of banking and nonbanking financial services. Mr. Anderson has also testified before the IRS and the Department of Labor on matters related to IRAs.

He is a graduate of Trinity College and the Stonier Graduate School of Banking at Rutgers. He is a member of numerous industry related associations, including being the president and board member of the Retirement Industry Trust Association (RITA).

Tom can be reached at:

PENSCO Trust Company
450 Sansome St, 14th Floor
San Francisco, CA 94111
1-415-274-5608 Direct
tom.anderson@pensco.com
www.penscotrust.com

Edwin Kelly

Director of Retirement Education Group, an affiliate of Equity Trust Company, Edwin Kelly is a recognized self-directed IRA expert and speaks to thousands of investors each year. Mr. Kelly works with professionals to help them gain a greater understanding of the advantages of self-directed investing, and he manages a group of retirement plan specialists. During the past 15 years, Mr. Kelly has worked with clients of different backgrounds and financial situations and has been a consultant to large financial institutions. Mr. Kelly holds Series 7 and Series 62 licenses with the National Association of Securities Dealers. He served on the board of directors of two nonprofit organizations. He is also an active real estate investor and holds his real estate license in the state of Ohio.

Mr. Kelly is a graduate of Franklin University, where he received a bachelor of science degree with an emphasis on finance, banking, and business management and a master's of business administration degree.

Edwin can be reached at:

**Equity Trust Company
225 Burns Rd.
Elyria, OH 44035
1-440-323-5491 Direct
e.kelly@trustetc.com
www.trustetc.com**

CHAPTER 1

Fear, Greed, and Your Retirement

Have you ever pictured what retirement would be like? Most people, usually during stressful days with endless phone calls and emails, have stared out the office window and envisioned the retired life. Perhaps your dreams include swaying palm trees on a quiet beach, the waves gently kissing the sand. Or perhaps your dream is gazing down the fairway of a championship golf course as you set yourself to tee off. No matter what dream of retirement you hold in your mind, it takes money to get there. Money to live in the lifestyle of your choosing, money for travel, and don't forget those greens fees!

Often the mention of cash virtually obliterates the wonderful image you had in your mind a moment earlier. A decided uneasiness settles upon most people when they think about how much they are actually saving for retirement or glance at the return they are getting on their investments right now. While the clock is ticking, we feel as if retirement is barreling toward us at lightning speed and fear that at our current pace of monetary accumulation, the island life or golf-course hopping is just a pipe dream.

Americans are living longer. Retirement ages are being pushed back. Employers are ending traditional pensions and cutting back on retiree health care. The future of Social Security remains uncertain. Sound scary? Not enough to kick Americans into high gear on their retirement savings, according to a new study called *The National Retirement Risk Index* from the Center for Retirement Research at Boston College. It shows that 43% of working-age households are at risk of being unable to maintain their current standard of living in retirement, up from 31% in 1983.

According to the Employee Benefit Research Institute, nearly 60% of workers have never bothered trying to figure out how much money they will need for retirement. That's a big problem. You cannot create a plan to reach your goal if you don't have a goal in mind. No one number suits everyone. Maybe you want to travel the world while your neighbor prefers to spend time at home with family. Nowhere is this fear of retirement more prevalent, with a healthy dose of denial, than within the baby boom generation.

The baby boom generation has produced a large bubble in the population, and this bubble is starting to retire. Comprising approximately 30% of the population, boomers are those individuals born between 1946 and 1964. They started retiring in 2005, and more than 4 million more will retire each year. They are facing an entirely different scenario than their parents did, and it is bringing the issues of retiring in today's current environment to the forefront.

Boomers' parents were the GI generation that survived the Great Depression and went to battle in World War II. They saved a large percentage of their money and had little opportunity or need for debt. When they retired, company pensions and Social Security combined with large savings accounts sustained them in their retirement years. Today, however, it's a different world.

Boomers are the first generation to have wide and varied access to consumer debt and a multitude of financial investments and instruments— in fact, they created them. However, they have not saved money like the generation before. Today most baby boomers have barely 25% of the savings their parents did at a similar age. The prevalent fear that they may run out of money or not be able to retire at all is certainly valid.

A survey conducted by Fidelity Investments in May 2007 found one in three workers have pushed back their expected retirement timetable due to financial shortfalls. Of those continuing to work, the reasons cited were:

- They have not saved enough for retirement (55%)

- They started saving for retirement too late (35%)

- They made poor investment choices or suffered from market fluctuations (27%)

Programs like Social Security and Medicare that have taken care of their parents may not be there for the boomers, and they know it. As the retiring population increases, it will put additional stress and strain on an outdated system. Social Security was never intended to serve as a pension plan. Additionally, when Social Security was enacted, the life expectancy was 62; now, it's over 78. That's a big gap and the only thing that will fill it is dollars!

For those who have invested in stocks over the years and accumulated a nest egg, frequent instability and erratic returns have made them nervous. Corporate scandals, war, and terrorist attacks can have devastating effects on investment accounts, and many investors have become disenchanted with the associated risk of a portfolio invested entirely in equities. Real estate is a wonderful way to diversify financially and moderate some of the volatility that might be experienced in the broader market. It also provides steady cash flow that can allow the investor the liquidity to purchase undervalued equities when there is a decline.

As interest rates have fallen in recent years, investors have also become very well acquainted with another obstacle to good returns—fees. In years past, when interest rates were high and the market soaring, fees were hidden in some of the highest returns in decades, but as rates have fallen, those same fees are taking a larger percentage, reducing average returns to very low levels. As boomers frantically try to make up financial ground, they are looking for investments that will be more advantageous and diversified.

Those generations following the boomers feel a sense of unease as well. Will they spend the next twenty years caring for their parents? How will they do that and still fund their own retirement?

Most people today put the bulk of the retirement savings into employer-sponsored plans. These include 401(k)s, profit sharing, 457 plans, 403(b)s, defined benefit plans, and many other types. Upon leaving their employer, most retirees roll their money out of these plans and into an individual retirement account (IRA). Most of these accounts that are administered by full-service banks or financial institutions offer a limited number of investment choices. These choices are composed of "traditional" investments, which include mutual funds, stocks, bonds, and other financial instruments. Following is a brief overview of the various types of IRAs you may have or be familiar with and the basics of how they work.

The IRA

An individual retirement account (IRA) is a wonderful way for people to save for their own retirement. An IRA allows the investor to save and invest money on a tax-deferred basis, which means no taxes are paid on the money contributed or its earnings until withdrawal, when presumably the investor could be in a lower tax bracket. The exception to this is the Roth IRA, in which contributions are made with money that is already taxed, and upon withdrawal, the principal and its earnings may be taken tax-free.

The effect of deferring the tax is the benefit of "compounded growth" on the full investment. Because you are not taxed until retirement, your return on investment is able to accumulate faster, and that accumulated interest may then also be reinvested. This concept applies to each of the various IRA types, although the tax implications and contribution rules vary among the accounts.

Traditional IRA and the rollover IRA

While the two types of accounts may potentially be merged, the difference in title refers to the way the IRA was originally funded.

Traditional IRA

The traditional deductible IRA was created for individuals who don't participate in an employer-sponsored retirement plan, although certain individuals who do participate in an employer-sponsored retirement program may still qualify for this IRA. The name implies that it has been or will be funded by cash contributions by the IRA owner. Income earned by your account is not taxable while it is in the account.

If you are under age 70½ and have earned income, or you have a spouse with qualifying earned income, you may each contribute up to $5,000 a year that may be tax-deferred. Individuals who attain the age of 50 before the close of the taxable year may contribute an amount in excess of the basic annual IRA contribution limit by $1,000 for a total of $6,000 a year (as of 2010).

The deadline for making a contribution is usually April 15 of the year following the desired contribution year (excluding extensions applicable to SEP IRAs only). Taxable distributions may be taken without penalty starting at age 59½ and must be started by April 1 once you have reached 70½.

Rollover IRA

A rollover IRA was designed as a holding account for funds distributed from a qualified retirement plan (401(k), 403(b), etc.). After 2002, it was no longer as necessary to maintain rollover IRAs. Now, funds rolled to any IRA from a qualified plan may be returned to another qualified retirement plan in the future.

Some plans require that you first establish you are receiving an IRA and provide them with the account number to facilitate the rollover. Transfers may be made to this account from another rollover IRA, traditional IRA, or pension plan.

The Roth IRA

Under the Taxpayer Relief Act of 1997, a new type of IRA, the Roth IRA, was established. Contributions to a Roth IRA are nondeductible, but if certain requirements are satisfied, all withdrawals from a Roth IRA will be free from income tax. Except as described below, a Roth IRA is treated like any other IRA.

To be treated as a Roth IRA, the IRA must be so designated when it is established. The maximum yearly contribution to all IRAs for the 2010 tax year is $5,000 ($6,000 for individuals who have attained age 50). Contributions to Roth IRAs and traditional IRAs are aggregated for purposes of applying these limits for both deductible and nondeductible contributions.

In order to make a full contribution to a Roth IRA for any year, a married taxpayer filing jointly must have joint adjusted gross income (AGI) of $159,000 (2010) or less for that year, and a single taxpayer must have AGI of $101,000 (2010) or less for that year. The AGI phase-out range (i.e., the range in which less-than-full contributions may be made) for Roth IRAs is between $150,000 and $160,000 for married taxpayers filing jointly and between $95,000 and $110,000 for single taxpayers.

Unlike traditional IRAs, an individual may contribute to a Roth IRA even after he or she has attained age 70½, provided he or she has earned income. Also, the age 70½ mandatory distribution requirements and the incidental benefit rules do not apply to Roth IRAs. Thus, no distributions are required until the IRA holder's death.

A traditional IRA may be rolled over or converted penalty free to a Roth IRA, provided that the individual's AGI (or joint AGI with his or her spouse) for the taxable year of rollover or conversion is not more than $100,000 and the individual is not married filing separately. Also, any rollover must be a "qualified rollover contribution," that is, a rollover contribution that meets the general IRA rollover rules, including the 60-day time limit rule. However, the rule that prohibits multiple IRA rollovers within a 12-month period does not apply.

Both deductible and nondeductible traditional IRAs may be converted or rolled over under these rules. Distributions from traditional IRAs will generally be taxable in the year of conversion or rollover to the extent they would otherwise be taxable if they were not part of a qualified rollover distribution. For purposes of the $100,000 limit, AGI is determined before any amount includable in income as a result of the conversion or rollover. Also, nondeductible contributions that are converted to Roth IRAs from traditional IRAs are not taxed.

"Qualified distributions" from a Roth IRA are excluded from ordinary income, which means that not only are they tax-free, but they also don't bump you into a higher tax bracket for your ordinary income. A qualified distribution is a distribution that is made after the five-taxable-year period that began with the first taxable year for which the individual (or the individual's spouse) made a contribution (including a rollover or conversion contribution from a traditional IRA) to the individual's Roth IRA and is:

- Made on or after the date the individual attains age 59½;

- Made to a beneficiary (or to the individual's estate) after the individual's death;

- A distribution attributable to the individual's being disabled; or

- A "qualified special purpose distribution" (which means a qualified first-time homebuyer distribution).

For example, Margie, who is 55, recently suffered the loss of her husband, who had a Roth IRA. Even though she is not 59½ yet, she may start receiving qualified nontaxable distributions from their Roth IRA. Another example might be a couple in their early thirties, Sam and Carol, who have been contributing to their Roth for several years. They are buying their first home and may receive a nontaxable and nonpenalized distribution of up to a lifetime limit of $10,000 under the "qualified special purpose" distribution clause to use for the purchase of that home.

SEP IRA

A SEP (Simplified Employee Pension) IRA is an employee benefit plan with compliance and reporting requirements simpler than those for qualified plans. For that reason, SEP IRAs are attractive for sole proprietors and small companies (up to 100 employees). Contributions (tax deductible to employers) must be made to IRAs because IRAs are the funding vehicle for SEPs. Contributions are limited to 25% of adjusted gross income or $41,000, whichever is less.

SEP participants can still contribute up to $5,000 (or $6,000 if over 50) to an IRA. However, because a SEP is an employee benefit retirement plan, an active participant in a SEP may not be able to deduct non-SEP contributions. The employer has until its tax filing date for its business, including any extensions, to make SEP contributions.

Investment options for IRAs

Many people are unaware that there is a wide array of investment options available for an IRA. This is due in part to the fact that many financial institutions offer a limited slate of investment vehicles for IRAs. When individuals see this limited slate, it is easy to assume that it represents all the investment vehicles that are possible. When IRAs were originally set up in 1974, the law was written to be exclusive rather than inclusive, which means that the law identified only those investments that could not be held in an IRA. This means that virtually everything else is fair game for investment under the tax code. Though you might assume that the list of prohibited investments is long, in reality there are only three items on the list:

1. **Collectibles—these include antiques, precious gems and metals, rugs, stamps or coins, works of art, and alcoholic beverages. There are exceptions for certain gold and silver coins minted by the U.S. Treasury.**

2. **Life insurance contracts—The investment of IRA funds into a life insurance contract on the life of the IRA owner or any other disqualified person is prohibited.**

3. **Subchapter S corporation stock—Investment in shares of an S corporation are not allowed because only certain trusts can be owners of an S corporation, and an IRA does not quality. If an IRA invests in shares of an S corporation, the status of the S corporation reverts to that of a C corporation.**

You can see that if these are the only prohibited types of investments in an IRA, then there is a wealth of possibilities open to the creative investor. Here is just a short list of possible investments in which you may invest your IRA funds:

- Real estate

- Real estate in foreign countries

- Limited liability corporations

- Private equity and private companies

- Trust deeds, land trust, and mortgages

- Tax liens and tax deeds

- Joint ventures

- A new business

- Lending

One alternative that is gaining ground within the marketplace is the self-directed IRA. "Self-directed" is not a legally defined term but an industry term for an account that allows the account holder to choose their own investments. According to the *Wall Street Journal*, approximately 97% of all retirement account assets are invested with banks, brokerages firms, mutual fund companies, and insurance companies. There are hundreds of types of investments you can choose from these firms, but you may be wondering why some options aren't on your financial institution's list. There are several reasons.

First let's look at the way large financial institutions make money. Most of them handle thousands or even millions of transactions each and every day, and they make money on each transaction. The majority, if not all, of these transactions are handled by computer. The ability to perform millions of similar transactions allows that institution to increase their transaction load and thereby increase profits. They have structured their IRA products to fit within their range of "typical" transactions. It doesn't make monetary sense for them to allow anything unusual or out of the ordinary as that would decrease overall profitability. You must remember that all financial institutions are in business to make money, not to offer the broadest range of investments for investors.

The financial services industry (banks, brokerages firms, insurance companies, mutual fund companies, financial planners) typically make money by selling a product such as a variable annuity, loaded mutual fund, life insurance policy, or stock on a commission basis. These firms also make money by borrowing your money and paying you a percentage return and loaning it to others at the institutional or retail level. These people are not giving guidance on placing something such as real estate into your IRA because that would mean you would be taking money away from these financial institutions. Most financial advisors don't address "out of the box" ideas because they haven't figured out how to make money on them, and they already make money by offering their traditional products.

Another reason you may be unaware of how self-directed IRAs work is that individuals and institutions that provide the majority of financial products to Americans know little, if anything, about these strategies. They receive their training from banks, investment firms, and brokerages that don't offer these options. They aren't given the opportunity to learn the strategies and techniques that will benefit their clients. Most financial advisors are too busy trying to accumulate assets under management or sell a commission product to want to take the time to learn a topic that may not earn them or their employer a fat profit. Think million-dollar bonuses on Wall Street.

With a self-directed IRA, retirement account funds can be invested in such nontraditional assets as mortgages, raw land, commercial buildings, vacation rentals, and multifamily homes, just to name a few. Keep in mind that you do not have to "cash out" your IRA to do this type of investing—these investments are made within a self-directed IRA. Rolling current retirement funds from an existing IRA or 401(k) account into a self-directed IRA to do this type of investing is penalty free.

The following is an example of how investing directly into real estate within a self-directed IRA can be a lucrative retirement strategy:

Sharon is interested in purchasing a duplex with her IRA funds. She found the property in her own community and the duplex is 100% occupied. The asking price is $200,000, but she only has $125,000 in her IRA. She is able to finance 50% with an IRA non-recourse loan specially designed for this type of transaction. Therefore, Sharon's IRA has directly funded 50% of the purchase price, and she has financed the remaining 50% with an IRA non-recourse loan of $100,000.

Rental income from the residential duplex now flows directly back to Sharon's IRA as a return on investment. Her IRA uses a portion of that income to pay off expenses related to the running and maintenance of the property, such as the monthly mortgage payment to the bank, insurance coverage, property taxes, maintenance, and repairs. At the end of the year, Sharon's IRA will have a net income of $4,000, after all expenses are paid. If the real estate then appreciates at an average of 4% per year, then that gain is in addition to the rental income.

Real estate is an investment that most people can understand in contrast to individual stocks, bonds, or other types of securities. Using your IRA, your real estate investment can include single-family homes, duplexes, fourplexes, or multifamily units. Best of all, you can invest in any real estate market you wish, including your hometown.

For investors who are looking for diversification of investments, the opportunity for better than average returns and a different way of securing their retirement, a self-directed IRA may be exactly what they have been seeking.

CHAPTER 2

How Your IRA Can Work for You

Saving for retirement on an individual basis came into the mainstream in 1974 when Congress passed a tax act known as the Employment Retirement Income Security Act (ERISA). Although ERISA was enacted primarily to regulate employer-sponsored plans, Congress also recognized that some employers would not sponsor pension plans, which left many Americans without access to the benefit of saving for retirement on a tax-deferred basis. To address this issue, Congress created individual retirement arrangements (IRAs) to encourage individual savings. Although there have been many changes and adjustments to the basic IRA structure originally enacted by Congress, the ability to self-direct your IRA into "nontraditional" assets has been available since the original act was passed in 1974. The following graphic shows the timeline of some of the more important changes to IRAs over the years:

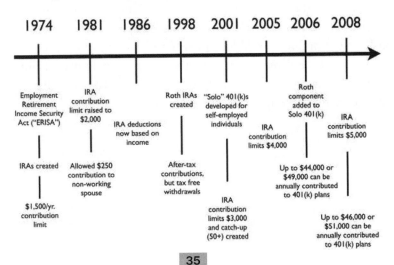

A self-directed IRA is legally no different from any other IRA. The term "self-directed" simply indicates that you choose your IRA's investments. Most brokerage houses and banks that offer what they call "self-directed" IRAs are often actually limited to that institution's scope of their own investment products. Self-directed IRA custodians or administrators that do not offer proprietary products have no need for this restriction, which means more options for the individual investor.

The rules governing the IRA investment options are exclusive, not inclusive. That is, the rules only specify where you *cannot* invest. Therefore, there is a virtually unlimited array of possible investments that fall well within the permissible boundaries. Self-directed IRAs offer investors tremendous flexibility in choosing investments for their retirement savings.

While most self-directed custodians accommodate traditional investments such as mutual funds and stocks, specialized companies also allow clients to invest in all forms of real estate (e.g., raw land, rental properties, commercial properties, and even real estate-related private entities, such as limited liability companies that invest in real estate). Some also specialize in investments called private placements, such as those associated with funding a startup company. Many people are shocked to learn that they can use the 401(k) from a former employer to help start a new business.

A 401(k) is an employer-sponsored pension plan that typically restricts the employees' investment choices to mutual funds and stocks. Pension plans that are self-directed typically place restrictions on investment choices and are often limited to the investment products offered by the custodian of that plan. Once you leave the employ of a company sponsoring a 401(k), you have the option to roll your plan benefits to a self-directed IRA. At that time, you can invest in whatever the new custodian permits. In many companies, when you reach the age of 59½, even if you are still employed with the company, you are permitted to roll over your 401(k) to a self-directed IRA.

Investing in real estate with your IRA

Real estate has become a very lucrative investment for many individuals over the last two decades. Those with money sitting in an IRA may have experienced the frustration of not being able to access that money to invest in the real estate market. What they don't realize is that they absolutely can invest in real estate with those funds.

The first step is to find a custodian or administrator who allows real estate transactions within a self-directed IRA. A short, and by no means conclusive list of IRA custodians and administrators is included in the back of this book. Once you have located the custodian or administrator that meets your needs, you can then transfer your existing IRA or roll over your pension plan accounts to a self-directed IRA. Once you find a property, you then instruct the custodian or administrator to make the deposit and the purchase. Instead of mutual funds or stocks, you'll have a rental property or ten acres in Missouri as part of your IRA portfolio.

This is not a new concept. The fact is that you have been able to buy real estate within your IRA account since the first day IRAs were created in 1974. While a small percentage of Americans have already benefited from this knowledge, it's not too late for you to take advantage of the opportunity as well.

Previously, the use of IRAs and other retirement plans to purchase real estate was an option that was not well-known. Things are changing rapidly due to the popularity of real estate investing and the recent press coverage of the self-directed IRA market.

Americans have become disillusioned with traditional investment choices and the lackluster results of their retirement investment activities. Recent economic and business events, such as the stock market decline, business scandals and corruption, and the burst of the dot-com bubble, along with low interest rates, have awakened passive investors whose retirement portfolios have suffered. They are ready to diversify their portfolio by adding real estate as an investment to reduce their risk of exposure in the stock market.

According to the Congressional Budget Office, American retirement savings lost more than $2 trillion due to stock market turmoil in the 14 months leading up to October 2008. This lost wealth may not be recovered for years. At the same time, real estate has been a stable long-term investment with cash returns and appreciation. Even during periods of decline in the real estate market, those assets still produce a steady stream of cash. In addition, of course, depressed real estate prices mean real estate is on sale, paving the way for future profits through appreciation.

Consequently, investors are now demanding that their brokers, bankers, and financial advisors provide information about alternative investments. Today's savvy investors want more control and tangible assets in their portfolios. They are tired of being at the mercy of the large institutional stock buyers and sellers. They are untrusting of large corporations following the series of recent collapses and scandals involving some of the most trusted names in finance such as Lehman Brothers, Bernie Madoff, and Bear Stearns.

Unfortunately, when seeking alternatives to restore retirement savings or attempting to diversify to reduce volatility, investors are frequently discouraged by their brokers, bankers, or advisors. You may hear some of the following comments from them, either out of their own ignorance or self-interest; they may say "You can't do that," or, "It's illegal," or, "We don't handle those types of investments," etc. In truth, some of these professionals have never been told that it is legal to buy real estate in an IRA. They don't know any better because the companies that employ them are not interested, or they never informed themselves.

Because brokers are compensated only when they sell stocks, bonds, and mutual funds, they are not trained in the details of performing real estate transactions.

Mutual funds (e.g., their company's funds), insurance companies (e.g., annuities or 403(b)s, and most securities brokers (e.g., stocks and bonds) make their money when you buy their investment products. They are not interested in having you buy a parcel of land and hold it for three years, because then you can't buy their investment products.

Traditional banks make money by using their clients' cash deposits, whether that's checking, savings, or time deposits such as certificates of deposit (CDs). In fact, they make so much money that they frequently charge little or no fees to administer your IRA, just so that you'll invest with them. There is clearly a place for the traditional bank. However, the investor should not be naive about why those institutions have a large number of branches and big marketing budgets.

The same is true of the large brokers, dealers, and mutual fund companies, although they are compensated differently. For example, some brokers can receive a one-time commission of up to 6% just for selling you a mutual fund and continue to receive fees (12b-1 fees) for as long as you own that fund. Clearly it is not in their best interest to allow you to use your IRA money to invest in real estate.

Why wouldn't these banks and institutions be willing to get into the self-directed IRA business? Because it just isn't as profitable as their primary business. Thus, there is no compelling reason for them to move into this market. They can't earn as much on this aspect of self-directed investing, and the cost of operations is higher because processing real estate investments is not automated. All of these traditional businesses rely, to a large degree, on electronic processing of financial transactions. They are not geared for a high volume of manual transactions. Nevertheless, as more Americans begin to self-direct, it is very likely that some of the traditional providers will enter the business, though it will be difficult for them to perform as well as companies that have specialized in this area for more than a decade.

It may seem that self-directed IRAs are the biggest investment secret out there today, and that's partially true. The small amount of, or nonexistent marketing of, these types of services has, in the past, been completely overshadowed by the large financial institutions. Because of their efficiency and profitability, traditional IRA providers control about 97% of the IRA industry. Their huge marketing budgets allow them to maintain a strong public presence, although recent articles in the national media are now giving much-needed exposure to the valuable self-directed service industry. This has started a groundswell of interest that will rapidly sweep across the country.

According to a study done by a large firm that administers self-directed IRAs, of the $4.6 trillion invested in IRAs as of 2008, only about $50 billion was allotted to self-directed IRAs, though the sector is growing at a rate of approximately 25% a year.

Is it really legal to buy real estate in an IRA?

Yes. Visit www.IRS.gov for confirmation directly from the Internal Revenue Service. Once there, perform a search for Publication 590 (a condensed version of Publication 590 is located in the Additional Resources section), which is the IRS booklet that defines everything the IRS wants you to know about IRAs. This includes a list of what you *can't* do within an IRA. You will see, as previously mentioned, that you cannot purchase collectibles or life insurance contracts.

You will also notice that real estate is not mentioned as one of the asset types in which an IRA is prohibited from investing. There is mention that you cannot borrow from an IRA, sell to your IRA, or use an IRA as security for a loan. Because that would create a prohibited transaction, many have felt that real estate investing would be a problem. This is true *if* you use your IRA as collateral for a loan that you, the IRA owner, personally guarantee. Clearly, under the tax laws, that is a prohibited transaction, just as borrowing $100,000 out of your IRA to buy a house would be a prohibited transaction. However, there are many other ways to buy real estate, as you will soon learn.

Also included in the resources section of this book is a list of companies that are aware of the legality and rules regarding investing in real estate with your IRA. You may contact any of them and discuss real estate investment in more detail.

Your IRA can purchase raw land, rental properties, commercial property, condominiums, mobile homes, boat slips, locomotives, earth-moving machines, race horses, cattle, tax liens, airplanes, tax certificates, foreign real estate, and billboards; start a business; buy mortgage notes; and loan money earning interest. All of these have to be handled strictly as investments and cannot be used personally. You must understand that anything purchased with your IRA funds is owned by your IRA, not by you personally. This is why the paperwork and purchases must be handled by a custodian or administrator. If you handle the transaction yourself, it would become taxable and you would lose the advantages of having the IRA in the first place.

As far as the IRS is concerned, buying 100 acres of raw land in Florida is just like buying 100 shares of IBM, a standard transaction for a self-directed IRA. Buying real estate is just a purchase of a different type of investment. The transaction execution is also quite different. Whereas the purchase of 100 shares of IBM can be performed instantaneously through the Internet, the completion of a real estate transaction takes place in many steps over a 30- to 60-day period. The careful handling of hundreds of real estate transactions simultaneously requires the effort of a specialized custodian or administrator.

Real estate IRA investing opens up a huge range of alternative investments for individuals who are knowledgeable about real estate investing or who work with knowledgeable advisors, sponsors, or brokers. Investing in real estate for your retirement may serve as a means to diversify your retirement portfolio to hedge against the cyclical changes in the stock market, economy, and bank and government-based investments.

For many who are experienced with real estate investing, real estate investments hold the potential to protect against the loss of principal while generating better than market-rate returns through income production and capital gains. When real estate investments are not leveraged, both income and capital gains can flow back to IRAs tax-deferred (or tax-free if the IRA is a Roth IRA).

If you have your IRA purchase real estate from an unrelated party and pay cash for it, and you do not use the real estate for personal reasons while it is in your IRA (i.e., you treat it strictly as an investment), there are no special issues.

If your IRA invests in real estate through a down payment and debt financing with a loan, there are some additional issues to consider:

- You cannot personally guarantee a loan for your IRA;

- It may be difficult to get a bank to allow an IRA to be the debtor without a personal guarantee. Currently, there are only a few banks that specialize in loans to self-directed IRAs nationwide. The minimum IRA down payment for such loans is 30–35%, although the exact down payment is dependent on the property, cash flow, current IRA balance, and market conditions.

- Your IRA may pay tax on unrelated debt-financed income (UDFI), which is the income and/or capital gains attributable to the leveraged portion. (UDFI is taxed at the trust tax rate because an IRA is treated as a trust for this purpose.) See chapters 5 and 6 for more details.

- As a consequence, although it is perfectly legal, it may not be desirable to have an IRA carry debt in a real estate investment transaction if there is any significant risk that the IRA will be unable to pay the mortgage.

What you can't do in an IRA with real estate

1. Your IRA cannot directly or indirectly buy real estate from a "disqualified person." Who is a disqualified person?

- The IRA owner;

- the IRA owner's spouse, descendant (e.g., son), or ascendant (e.g., mother);

- spouse of a descendant of the IRA holder; or

- a fiduciary of the IRA or person providing services to the IRA (e.g., the trustee or custodian).

2. Your IRA cannot be the principal participant in an investment for yourself or another disqualified person. In other words, if the IRA's investment is deemed essential to accomplishing a transaction in which both you and your IRA invest, then the transaction would be considered a prohibited transaction.

3. Your IRA cannot purchase a real estate asset and then have a disqualified person use it while it is in the IRA. For example, you cannot buy a vacation home and use it partly for personal use, even though you might rent it to unrelated persons the rest of the year.

The easiest way to grasp the way an IRA functions in these situations is to understand that the IRA is working as its own independent entity— picture in your mind that it is not a part of you, an extension of you, or an asset of yours. You only benefit when the money is withdrawn according to the IRA rules set up by the government. Anytime you step outside those rules, or try to commingle the IRA assets with your own in any way, you can run into trouble. (See chapter 9 on prohibited transactions for a more detailed explanation.)

What you can do in an IRA with real estate

Buying real estate from an unrelated party (i.e., one who is not a disqualified person) with cash is the simplest way of investing in real estate with your IRA. Your IRA can buy raw land, commercial property, residential (e.g., rental) property, and real estate options, as well as extend loans (e.g., first and second mortgages), secured by real estate with your IRA, to unrelated parties.

As discussed earlier, your IRA can also buy property through leveraging, provided the loan is not guaranteed by the IRA owner (or any other disqualified person) and that the IRA has enough rental income to support the mortgage and expenses. In the event you have a rental property vacancy, you should have liquidity in the IRA to cover the expenses.

There is a variety of ways, however, that an IRA can participate in a real estate investment without a full cash capital investment. For example, your IRA can co-invest with other parties. You could also have your IRA and other parties participate in real estate investing by becoming members of an LLC that buys and sells property.

CHAPTER 3

Financial Planning and Your IRA

Eric Wikstrom, CPA, CFP®

In the previous chapters, we've talked about the self-directed IRA and some of the possibilities it offers to take advantage of different types of investments. Whether it is real estate, deeds of trust, business start-ups, or anything else allowed by law, your IRA can probably invest in it. While it is exciting to consider these options, it is important to step back and consider where this type of investment fits into your overall financial plan.

The reason for taking this extra time to seriously consider what you want is relatively straightforward: if you don't make some decisions up front, you might find yourself becoming involved in all types of investments that don't really suit your personality or risk tolerance. While a particular investment may be perfect for your brother or your golf buddy, that doesn't mean it will suit you. On top of general suitability for a particular investment, you also have to understand that when you invest within an IRA, the situation is very different than investing outside an IRA and involves gaining certain knowledge about taxation and daily operations.

It is not uncommon for an investor to hear about oil and gas partnerships, mineral rights investing, or any of a number of other opportunities and think they can make a fortune. Before you undertake any investment, it is important to run the investment opportunity through your own "investment filter" to ascertain if it fits within the predetermined investment profile that you will have created for your IRA. While it may be tempting to jump at every "can't miss" opportunity that comes along, a lack of planning ahead can ultimately leave you with what I call the "Box of Chocolates" portfolio—one of everything and nothing that really performs or meets your long-term needs.

Investor psychology

Before we get too far down the path of understanding the nuts and bolts of how particular investments work, it is critical to first understand your investor psychology, which includes who you are as an investor, what your life situation is, and what stage you are at in your investment timeline.

Without making too many assumptions, it is probably safe to assume that almost everyone would enjoy more wealth rather than less. There may be individuals out there who are uncomfortable with great wealth, but for the purposes of this exercise, we'll operate on the assumption that everyone prefers more wealth over less. We will also work with the understanding that wealth creation is a journey, not an overnight event or a one-time shot. Unless you inherit a great deal of money or win the lottery, it's unlikely that your IRA will grow from $2,000 to $1,000,000 immediately with one investment.

Wealth building, for most of us, is a life-long endeavor and takes a great deal of time and patience. This is why it is important to understand up front who you are as an investor and what your goals are. You also must know what kind of investment psychology you have. For example, are you a risk taker who is not afraid to lose your entire investment, or does the act of opening your monthly brokerage statement make your stomach tense up? It is this investor psychology, and yours in particular, that is important to understand. In order to feel comfortable with your investments and sleep at night, you need to have the types of investments that suit your particular investor psychology.

A very wise man once said, "People are funny about money—theirs in particular." After many years of working with individuals and their finances, I find that phrase rings true. Most people can talk about investments in an abstract and unemotional way. However, when it's their money on the line, things are different; understanding why that difference occurs is a key component to understanding your own investor psychology.

Past history with money

We are all products of our environment, and this history often plays a large part in how we view our money and our investing. If there were periods in your childhood or adult career where earning money or accumulating savings was a challenge, these past events will most likely have a significant effect on how you treat money as an adult and, more specifically, how you view your investments.

The area where your investor psychology is often most evident is in the area of investment returns. When I review the performance of portfolios with clients, I notice that their reactions, stress, and agitation are usually a function of their prior history with money, along with their current life situation. Most investors experience a higher level of disappointment from a negative 10% portfolio return than they do enjoyment from a positive 10% return. While no one likes to lose money or have negative investment returns, if the fact that you *might* lose money on an investment keeps you up at night, you need to be concerned about the types of investments you put into your IRA.

Investments such as cash, CDs, U.S. Treasury Bills, and other very liquid investments will usually ensure that you get your principal back with some return on your investment and are therefore considered very safe. However, very conservative investments have their problems as well. These investments often struggle just to keep up with inflation, and the fact that people are living longer may mean that you must seek higher returns in order to have enough money to last through retirement. Investing is a balance of protecting what you have and growing that money enough to meet your long-term needs. This means that the right balance for you will be different from the next person and may also change as you age and your life circumstances change.

Money personality

Everyone has a "money personality." This personality forms the framework of how you view money: the accumulation of it, the spending of it, and the giving of it. For many people, their money personality is often a function of their current career. People who have been, and currently are, successful entrepreneurs or investors are usually more comfortable with risk because they believe they can make back any losses relatively quickly should the need arise. These people have a tendency to be more aggressive as investors.

Employees making a fixed wage who are going to continue in their career choice for the immediate future have a tendency to be more conservative. This is because it has taken them longer to accumulate money and they realize that if they lose it, it will take many years to accumulate again.

Another large factor in anyone's money personality is how they view their estate distribution when they die. Some people want to die with only one nickel left in their pocket, knowing that they had the best time they could while alive and leave nothing behind. Others want to pass on a considerable "estate" to family, friends, and charities.

This estate distribution viewpoint will usually be a large determining factor in how individuals invest, especially with their IRA funds.

Risk and return

The reason that it is so important to spend some time understanding your money psychology is that investing is like the old saying, "There's no such thing as a free lunch." In other words, in order to get a higher return, you need to take on more risk and create a balance that suits your risk tolerance and also achieves your goals. There are no returns without some risk and the higher the return, the higher the risk. You never get one without the other; there are no exceptions.

The graphic on page 49 shows examples of some investments along this risk/return continuum.

The Risk/Return Continuum

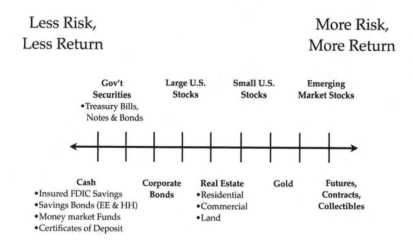

Less Risk,
Less Return

More Risk,
More Return

| Gov't Securities | Large U.S. Stocks | Small U.S. Stocks | Emerging Market Stocks |

•Treasury Bills, Notes & Bonds

| Cash | Corporate Bonds | Real Estate | Gold | Futures, Contracts, Collectibles |

•Insured FDIC Savings
•Savings Bonds (EE & HH)
•Money market Funds
•Certificates of Deposit

•Residential
•Commercial
•Land

As you can see, in order to make intelligent investment choices you'll need to have a firm understanding of your risk tolerance and money psychology. Otherwise, you'll either be creating an IRA portfolio that contains much more risk than you realize and with more volatility as well, or one that isn't likely to keep pace with inflation and your retirement needs.

Portfolio creation

In the risk/return continuum, we looked at different types of investments and their corresponding risk and return levels. These different types of investments are more commonly known as asset classes within the financial world. Asset classes are types of investments that are grouped according to similar characteristics. For example, stocks of large U.S. companies are grouped together, as are international stocks. This allows investors to choose investments that meet their goals because they know the risk/return category of a particular investment. But even when the assets are grouped, you still must determine how they will function together in a portfolio and how much of each asset is right for you. This is known as asset correlation.

What is asset correlation and how does it work?

Choosing a certain percentage of different asset classes (such as stocks and bonds) that move up and down under different market conditions helps you offset the falling returns of one asset class with an increase in another. This basic strategy of mixing different asset classes helps you lower the risk of your entire portfolio as you protect against big losses, putting you in a position to achieve better overall portfolio performance.

Statistically speaking, correlation captures the linear relationship between two variables. In portfolio management theory, correlation shows whether, and how strongly, selected assets are related. It measures the strength of the historical relationship between two investments by measuring how much the returns of any two or more investments are related. But correlation does not imply that the movement of one investment causes the movement of another, or that this relationship will continue in the future. Correlation ranges from +1.0 to -1.0, where +1.0 equals perfect positive correlation, -1.0 equals perfect negative correlation, and 0.0 equals zero correlation. Following is a correlation matrix that shows the correlations between various commonly held asset classes.

4Q ROLLS: 1990 Q1 THROUGH 2006 Q2 (EXC. HEDGE FUNDS START 1994 Q4)							
	# Periods	Bonds	Stocks	Real Estate	Commod- ities	Private Equity	Hedge Funds
Bonds	66	1.00	0.00	-0.39	-0.23	-0.25	0.04
Stocks	66	0.00	1.00	0.05	-0.03	0.74	0.64
Real Estate	66	-0.39	0.05	1.00	0.08	0.09	0.04
Commod- ities	66	-0.23	-0.03	0.08	1.00	0.26	0.35
Private Equity	66	-0.25	0.74	0.09	0.26	1.00	0.59
Hedge Funds	47	0.04	0.64	0.04	0.35	0.59	1.00

Correlation data is based on the returns of the following market indices - Bonds: Lehman Aggregate; Stocks: Russell 3000; Real Estate: NCREIF-NPI; Commodities: GS Commodity Index; Private Equity: Venture Economics U.S. Private Equity; Hedge Funds: C.S. Tremond Hedge Fund Index.

Now look at the correlation between stocks and real estate. These two asset classes have a +0.05 correlation, which indicates that the return of stocks or real estate have almost no correlation to the return of the other. When real estate is up 10%, stocks generally would be up 0.5%. Again this is not the result of cause and effect. It is the correlation of two asset classes to the same set of market conditions.

Correlation, asset allocation, and diversification

Since we can use correlation to improve diversification and reduce portfolio risk, it is important to know when and how it reduces risk to be sure we diversify beneficially.

When you combine two or more investments with perfect positive correlation, in theory, there is no reduction of portfolio risk. The risk of the resulting portfolio is simply an average of the individual risks of the two or more investments. If you continue to add more investments with perfect correlation, the portfolio will continue to produce an average return without reducing risk. For example, if you own bonds, and you add more bonds, this does not reduce overall risk. You just earn the average of all the bonds you hold and still have the same risk.

If you combine two or more investments that have zero correlation, portfolio risk may be reduced, because the investments move independently and are statistically unrelated. A good example of this would be stocks and bonds. If you add more uncorrelated investments to the portfolio, you may be able to reduce risk, but not eliminate it completely.

If you combine two or more investments with perfect negative correlation, you could eliminate risk altogether for a portfolio. An example of this might be a CD and an interest bearing savings account. Your money would be safe and secure, but this would also have a negative effect on your return and prevent you from reaching your investment goals. Generally, the lower the risk of an investment, the lower the return.

You must decide what your financial goals are and how you want your portfolio to perform before you start investing. Knowing how particular investments are correlated to major market indexes will help you build a more balanced portfolio that will give you results you can understand and live with. Keep this portfolio balancing act in mind before you add any additional investment to your portfolio mix, whether it is in your IRA or taxable portfolio.

Asset allocation

Diversification helps you avoid placing all your bets on one asset class, multiple asset types, or classes that are highly correlated. Modern portfolio theory has proven that the use of multiple asset classes or asset types that are not highly correlated or are negatively correlated is the best way to protect and build an investment portfolio. Unfortunately, most Americans' retirement accounts are in the public stock market either in the form of stocks or mutual funds. This makes their portfolios susceptible to overall swings in the stock market; this risk is called a "systemic" risk.

Diversifying into a variety of noncorrelated asset types and/or classes (groups of similar asset types) is generally the best way to grow your retirement portfolio. Self-directed IRAs provide the freedom to diversify into a wide array of asset types. However, it will still be up to you or your appointed advisor to decide how to allocate your mix of assets. For example, suppose, after you read this book, you decide to include real estate in your retirement portfolio along with some stocks, bonds, and time deposits. How much of each do you choose?

By now you probably realize that constructing your portfolio with 90% stocks and mutual funds, 5% real estate and 5% time deposits won't do much to protect you from a systemic decline in the stock market. But how much do you "allocate" to each of these asset types? Well, this is a dynamic process that should take into consideration the current performance of each asset class and its expected performance going forward. For example, those who invested in real estate from 2001 through 2006 generally did a lot better than those who invested in the stock market over the same period. There was no dot-com bomb in the real estate industry until 2008. But the stock market, surprisingly, was also simultaneously affected by the global economic crisis that impacted all but a few asset classes (e.g., precious metals and gold). Savvy investors may have "reallocated" their investment portfolios at the beginning of this global crisis into asset classes that were not or were negatively correlated to the areas of decline. Gold is an asset type that generally declines in a strong economy with a strong U.S. dollar and appreciates when the economy and dollar decline. Cash and time deposits tend to preserve capital by eliminating exposure to loss. It is, therefore, important to pay attention to your asset allocation and to adjust it as financial conditions change over time.

Where do your investment funds come from?

Investing as it relates to individuals can be simply stated: you have two pockets—a taxable pocket and a tax-advantaged pocket. Your taxable pocket is simply where you store most of the assets that you touch and deal with on a regular basis. A checking and savings account, CDs, an investment brokerage account, investment real estate, automobiles, personal property, personal residence—these are examples of assets that we'll include in your taxable pocket. These are "taxable" assets because you previously paid tax on the dollars used to acquire these assets. Because they are in the taxable pocket, there may be *current tax consequences* to buying or selling any of these assets.

The tax-advantaged pocket is the "other" pocket. Investments that you'll find here include your traditional IRA, Roth IRA, SEP or Simple IRA, workplace 401(k) plan, Solo 401(k) plan, defined benefit plan, 403(b), and other plans. Basically, any IRA or qualified retirement plan will be included in this pocket.

Once you understand that investment options are limited to one of these two pockets, the question to ask is, "In *which pocket* should I own real estate, mutual funds, private equity investments, business interests, variable annuities, etc.?" You only have two choices to own anything: in a currently taxable environment (your taxable pocket) or a tax-deferred or tax-free environment (your tax-advantaged pocket). It's really that simple. It doesn't even matter what type of entity or structure you utilize to make your investment. A trust, LLC, partnership, or C corporation are all options.

Simply stated, if the end result is that the gain or loss on annual operations or ultimate sale of the asset finds its way to your individual tax return, then consider it held in your taxable pocket. If the same gain or loss on operations or on sale does not get taxed to you today, but either at some point in the future—or better yet, never—then these investments are in your "other" pocket, your tax-advantaged pocket.

The key point is to make sure you have all the correct information before you determine which pocket to make your investment in because your retirement pocket might be the best place to make an investment due to a variety of personal factors that are unique to only you. Don't let financial commentators sway you into not making a great investment due to *their opinion* or conventional financial wisdom. Your situation is completely unique and investing is not a one-size-fits-all proposition.

Taxes and your pockets

There is a great deal of misinformation in the financial press about making certain types of investments in or outside of an IRA. The misinformation is because few individuals know or understand the ultimate result that most transactions have on your total tax picture. Many tax practitioners will tell clients that they should not purchase leveraged (financed with a loan) real estate in their IRA because they might pay some unrelated business income tax (UBIT). I find that is usually just an uninformed comment made by someone who doesn't practice in the area of individual taxation or who doesn't understand how the Internal Revenue Code actually works.

We will talk about UBIT in a later chapter, but in a nutshell, if your IRA uses debt to finance the purchase of real estate, your IRA *may* owe some tax based on the amount of income that is derived from the amount of debt financing used to purchase the real estate. Just the thought of the IRA owing tax in and of itself is enough to make most tax practitioners squirm. Consequently, rather than seeking to understand how UBIT actually works in this situation, they advise clients not to purchase real estate in their IRAs. But as the following analysis shows, chances are you'll pay less in income taxes if your IRA pays the taxes as opposed to paying the taxes out of your taxable pocket for the same investment.

The two following examples below show how a real estate investment that generates $10,000 and $100,000 of taxable income (rental income less depreciation, interest, property taxes, etc.) will actually pay less in income taxes if the investment is made in an IRA versus outside an IRA using taxable funds.

	Investment held in IRA	Investment held outside IRA	Investment held in IRA	Investment held outside IRA
Regular Taxable Income	N/A	$10,000	N/A	$100,000
Gross Income from Debt Financed Property	$10,000	N/A	$100,000	N/A
Debt % applied to income	50%	N/A	50%	N/A
Income before special deduction	$5,000	$10,000	$50,000	$100,000
Specific UBIT deduction	-$1,000	N/A	-$1,000	N/A
Taxable Income	$4,000	$10,000	$49,000	$100,000
Applicable/Effective Tax Rate	20%	28%	33%	28%
Income Tax	$800	$2,800	$16,229	$28,000

As you can see, the total taxes owed with the real estate owned by the IRA are substantially less than if you owned the real estate with your taxable funds. Not only that, but there is a great deal of additional peripheral damage that is also incurred if you own real estate with your taxable funds. The table on the following page examines the effect on your taxable pocket and your tax-advantaged pocket if positive rental income is generated from your real estate investment. This compares rental income outside an IRA and rental income from real estate held within an IRA.

Item	Taxable Pocket	Tax-Advantaged Pocket
Rental income	Increases AGI (adjusted gross income)	No effect
Alternative minimum tax	Increases AGI	No effect
Itemized deductions	Potentially reduces benefit of deductions with higher AGI	No effect
Standard deduction	Potentially reduces benefit of deductions with higher AGI	No effect
College financial aid	Greater income; greater net worth	No effect
Annual compliance costs	Increased compliance burden	Potential Form 990-T Requirement if UBIT

As you can see, the income itself, when held outside the IRA in the taxable pocket, can increase your AGI, which can limit your ability to contribute to an IRA for retirement. But income from property held in that IRA has absolutely no effect on your AGI allowing you to continue contributions as long as your income is below the AGI limits.

When you look at the alternative minimum tax, rental income that is held in the taxable pocket increases your AGI, which could make the alternative minimum tax go into effect. Of course this isn't an issue when held in the nontaxable pocket.

When your AGI increases as it would with rental income in the taxable pocket, then it can also reduce your standard and itemized deduction amounts—not so if the income is in the nontaxable pocket.

The only area to be aware of when rental income is derived from the nontaxable pocket is that there is a possibility that a Form 990-T *might* be required. This is only if the UBIT comes into play, which it can in some situations.

It is important to be fully informed and aware of your total tax picture and understand how any investment will be tax-affected. Don't just accept the conventional or standard advice from financial advisors that IRA investing doesn't have tax benefits, because it does.

Tax-deferred versus tax-free

We now understand that we have access to two pockets of money for making investments: your taxable pocket and your tax advantaged pocket. But one more concept needs further defining: tax-deferred versus tax-free. Tax-deferral means just what it says—the deferral or payment at a later date of taxes incurred on some event today.

Most retirement plans are tax deferred. Traditional IRAs, SEP IRAs, SIMPLE IRAs, and 401(k) plans fall into this category. The current earnings on the investments inside these retirement accounts are not currently taxed, but instead are deferred and taxed at some point in the future. This is extremely important due to what is known as the time value of money. This means that your money works for you over time and it is important to take advantage of the time value of money on a tax-deferred basis whenever you can. If you can invest money today and let the earnings grow for many years without losing some each year to income taxation, this compounding effect can truly be significant.

The only concept better than tax-deferred is tax-free. A tax-free situation currently only happens in a type of retirement account known as a Roth IRA or a Roth 401(k). Roth IRAs were created in 1998, and Roth 401(k)s were added in 2006. These types of retirement accounts are funded with after-tax dollars, not pretax dollars like in the tax-deferred accounts mentioned above.

In tax-deferred accounts (depending upon the type of account), you may qualify to have the amount of your annual contribution deducted from your earned income for current income tax purposes. Roth accounts are funded with your after-tax dollars. One of the best features of Roth accounts is that as long as the accounts have been open at least five years, they are tax *free*. Not tax-deferred, but tax *free*.

While Roth accounts are wonderful, there are certain income limitations that determine who can contribute to Roth IRAs and convert traditional IRAs to Roths, but with some reasonable tax planning, most of these obstacles can be overcome.

Other IRA financial planning considerations

Liquidity

Depending upon your age and the amount of other assets you have, liquidity in your IRA may or may not be an important concern. Liquidity basically means how quickly and easily your investments can be converted into cash. Because of all the uncertainties with the sale of real estate, conversion is usually not very easy nor can the account quickly be converted into cash. Keep in mind that you can always utilize your IRA investments. The amount of tax you will pay will vary based on age and type of IRA account you may have (traditional versus Roth, etc.), but it's your money and you can spend it as you wish.

Should a personal need arise that requires access to your IRA account, just keep in mind that the liquidity of your investments will determine how quickly you can get to your cash.

Investment policy statement

An investment policy statement is commonly used by institutional money managers to provide guidelines as to how much of any investment a manager can purchase.

The reason I mention it here is because understanding historical asset returns, volatility, and correlations are important factors in constructing a cohesive investment portfolio. Putting guard rails around the amount of stocks, bonds, or real estate in your portfolio is a good idea to keep you grounded and focused on building a diversified portfolio. It also prevents you from getting too far into one type of investment that can cause huge losses. The late 1990s were a great example of this; both individual investors and professional money managers got caught up in the large and small growth stock craze. The returns were great until the growth craze ended and the market corrected quickly. Because most investors didn't adjust their allocations frequently, the growth meant that the percentage of their entire portfolio held in these growth stocks had grown to a massive amount. During the large stock correction in the year 2000, these people suffered huge losses.

Having a document like an Investment Policy Statement can be a useful tool to remind you, regardless of the current market environment, how you intend to successfully meet your retirement goals.

Age

Conventional wisdom (and the financial press) tells investors that as they age and get closer to retirement their portfolios should become more and more conservatively invested. This is largely due to the fact that older individuals don't have the ability to go back to work and replenish their retirement accounts should they suffer large losses. Because of this advice, I frequently see older investors hold significant amounts of cash as they age. This is not necessarily bad or wrong as long as they understand that it is costing them. Two of the most fearful prospects for any investor are inflation and longevity.

The problem with inflation is that it eats into purchasing power. Constructing a very conservative portfolio in your later years means that cash returns usually don't keep up with inflation. Combine this with the fact that individual life expectancy is constantly increasing, and it becomes clear that getting conservative with a retirement portfolio in your sixties can cause you to run out of money if you end up living well into your eighties.

No matter whether you choose real estate or stocks, both of which have been shown to be good long-term inflation hedges, it is important to consider exactly how conservative you can become with your portfolio without making it subject to the damages of inflation and longevity.

Temperament

As we discussed previously in investor psychology, if your temperament is such that you don't cope well with swings in your portfolio's value, you probably need to do one of two things: (1) have a simply constructed portfolio that doesn't suffer much volatility, or (2) do not look at your portfolio very often (not a recommended idea).

The same goes for complexity. If you do not like the idea of keeping track of your investments on a regular basis, you need to understand this tendency and construct a managed portfolio that will adjust for your age and life changes without you having to do much. You can pay someone to do this for you directly or pay a mutual fund manager to do this by investing in an age-based investment product. But building a Rip Van Winkle portfolio (constructed once and never reviewed) is probably not advisable if you want to truly maximize your portfolio's potential and steer clear of problems.

Know what you own and know why you own it

You don't need to become an investment expert to ask intelligent questions. But at a basic level, you need to know what you own and why you own it. This may be the allocation of a small cap value mutual fund or the purchase of real estate. But if you can't answer the basic question of what you own and why you own it, shed that investment and start over.

Getting organized and developing a plan of action

Getting organized from an investment standpoint basically means developing an asset allocation plan and perhaps an investment policy statement. Unless you have given some thought to what you want your portfolio to look like, it is extremely easy to buy a little of this and a little that, all with good intentions.

This problem gets compounded with a husband and wife portfolio. Put together a joint taxable portfolio with a husband's IRA and a wife's 401(k), and without at least some planning, you end up with the Box of Chocolates portfolio. It is very rare that this "one of everything" portfolio will help you accomplish your goals. Think of your investment universe in terms of your two pockets, and things will become clearer on where to own certain types of investments.

Tax-efficient versus tax-inefficient

Most investments have a very pronounced tax profile. Hedge-fund managers trade their holdings frequently, so the gains generated from these funds usually consist of short-term capital gains, that is, ordinary income treatment. Real estate may generate some ordinary rental income and then the capital gain in the future when it is sold. This means that the investment is essentially taxed in two ways: as income for the rental money each year and then at the sale of the property for the capital gain. For this reason, real estate is considered tax-inefficient. Tax-inefficient investments make great choices for retirement accounts because of the tax deferral nature of the retirement account. Since the money that would go toward taxes stays in the account, it compounds and grows faster.

Some investments, like municipal bonds, are very tax-efficient because no federal (or perhaps state) income taxes are owed due to their special tax treatment. These types of investments are especially tax efficient when held in a taxable portfolio.

Knowing the tax profile of any investment will help you decide on which investment pocket to choose for your investing.

CHAPTER 4

The IRA Non-Recourse Loan

Once you make the decision that investing in real estate with the money in your IRA is for you, then it is important to know the options available to gain the best return possible. In the past, mortgage companies and banks were hesitant to lend money for investments within an IRA because the account owner could not personally guarantee the loan due to IRS regulations. This meant that most real estate investments using IRA funds were outright cash purchases. Therefore, if you wanted to buy a property for $100,000, you would need $100,000 in available IRA funds to make the purchase, which limits your potential returns.

Anyone familiar with real estate investment knows that leverage, or the use of debt financing, gives the investor the ability to stretch their available cash and substantially increase their return. This led North American Savings Bank to create a new product specifically suited to the IRA real estate investor called an IRA non-recourse loan.

A non-recourse loan can be used to leverage real estate held in the following self-directed entities:

- **IRA**

- **LLC (IRA owns shares of the LLC)**

- **Self-directed 401(k)**

- **Solo 401(k)**

- **C corporation**

- **Partnership**

- **Profit-sharing plans**

The loan is called *non-recourse* because it allows no recourse against the individual account holder or the balances of the IRA funds. In the event of default or foreclosure, the lender can only look to the property and leases as the sole source of repayment. The non-recourse lender cannot pursue other assets owned by the account holder or the IRA. This means that the only asset attached to the loan is the property itself and no other funds or guarantees can be used by the account holder as collateral for the loan.

When purchasing real estate in your personal name, you normally sign a personal guarantee on the promissory note (although a few states such as California do not allow lenders to hold the borrower personally liable for any deficiency between the loan balance and the value of the collateral at the time of foreclosure).

A *recourse* loan allows the lender to pursue any of your assets if the lender cannot recover its losses from the sale of the property in a foreclosure. Banks prefer a recourse loan over a non-recourse loan because the borrower has more to lose in the event of default.

You can visit Publication 590 at www.irs.gov to verify this specific requirement for non-recourse debt financing. We included a condensed version of the publication in the back of the book. Publication 590 states that an IRA "cannot be used as security for a loan," meaning that funds in the IRA cannot secure the loan. Thus a *non-recourse* loan is required to finance property within an IRA.

Up until 2004, IRA real estate investors either had to use 100% IRA funds to purchase the property outright as already described, or they had to acquire a hard-money loan to leverage the purchase. Hard-money lenders are typically individuals and are often unregulated. They typically require higher rates, larger origination fees, and shorter terms (a one- to two-year balloon). Because of these stipulations, hard-money loans rarely made sense for the investor looking to leverage real estate in an IRA.

It's extremely hard to find a lender who will entertain a non-recourse loan, especially in today's lending environment. Both large corporate banks and small local banks most likely are unfamiliar with a non-recourse loan or will not offer this type of financing because of the increased risk, or because they simply do not have the expertise to properly structure these transactions in compliance with IRS regulations. Most banks are comfortable with a personal guarantee on top of a lien against the property, so it's hard to break those traditional lending practices.

A non-recourse lender such as North American Savings Bank will hold 100% of these loans in their own portfolio because there is no secondary market for the sale of these mortgages. Banks normally bundle secondary market eligible loans for sale to Fannie Mae and Freddie Mac or other investors, which frees up the bank's working capital to make more loans. A non-recourse lender will hold these loans until they are paid off by the borrower, typically in 15 to 25 years. It is important to make sure you choose a non-recourse lender who understands the IRS rules and specializes in this type of loan.

The benefit of using this type of debt financing is that all net proceeds go back into the IRA tax-free and can be used to leverage real estate or other investments suitable for your IRA. Many people like the ability to add real estate to their IRA as a way to diversify their investments and, through leverage, the IRA account holder can use a percentage or portion of the available funds for the down payment rather than pay cash for the entire purchase price of the property.

Difference in qualifying

Qualifying for a non-recourse loan is quite different from qualifying for a conventional loan used for the typical purchase of a new home. A non-recourse lender *will not* look at the following when making their loan decision:

1. Your income

2. Your employment

3. W-2's

4. Tax returns

5. Assets outside your IRA, SEP, 401(k) accounts

Removing these variables can make the loan process simpler for both the lender and the borrower. A non-recourse loan is not reflected on your credit report under your Social Security number. Instead, the non-recourse loan closes under the tax ID number of the IRA or entity purchasing the property. This is very helpful if you are an experienced investor who owns multiple properties under your personal name. Fannie Mae and Freddie Mac limit the number of properties you can finance with conforming rates in your own name. Owning properties in your IRA will not count toward the number of properties purchased in your name and will not affect the debt-to-income ratio banks use when qualifying for a conventional loan.

A non-recourse loan is underwritten very similarly to a commercial real estate loan. The main concern for the lender is the property, the leases, cash flow, and equity. There are three main components non-recourse lenders will consider when making their decision:

1. Property—Is the property in rentable condition? Remember that 100% of the collateral for this type of loan is the real estate. So the lender must be satisfied with the value, marketability, and condition of the property at the time of closing. It's harder for a lender to sell a single-family home following a foreclosure if the home is in distressed condition versus rentable condition.

2. Cash flow—Does the property generate enough cash flow to cover the mortgage and expenses for the investment? I'll help you find these numbers later in this chapter, but it is a key factor in the bank's decision-making process.

3. IRA funds—The lender will verify that the IRA has enough funds for the down payment, closings costs, prepaid costs for real estate taxes and insurance, and reserves for any vacancies or repairs that may arise. All mortgage payments and expenses must come from the IRA. The IRS will not allow you to pay any mortgage payments or expenses from your personal funds.

North American Savings Bank provides non-recourse loans to real estate investors who have a minimum 30% to 40% of the purchase price plus reserves in a self-directed IRA or self-directed retirement plan. Non-recourse financing is subject to approval, including an acceptable real estate appraisal, as determined by the lender. As of 2010, the only lender providing financing for eligible properties within an IRA in all 50 states is North American Savings Bank (www.iralending.com). While the down payment for the purchase comes directly from the IRA, it is not considered an IRA distribution because the funds used for the down payment are going toward the purchase of an asset held in the IRA account.

Minimum down payment requirements vary depending on the lender and the type of property being considered for purchase. The following are some examples:

*   **Single-family homes— 30–35%**

*   **Two- to four-unit properties— 40%**

*   **Condominiums— 40–50%**

*   **Multifamily units (for five or more families)— 40%**

Property eligibility

Lenders will have their own requirements for the types of real estate they are willing to finance within your retirement account. It is important to remember that the property eligibility requirements are not IRS guidelines. Rather, they are bank guidelines and can vary from lender to lender. For example, North American Savings Bank considers the following properties to be eligible for their non-recourse loan program:

- Single-family residential

- Warrantable condos*

- Planned unit developments (PUDs)/townhomes

- Duplexes

- Fourplexes

- Multifamily (five or more units)

*Warrantable condos include those:

- That are 100% complete including common areas and individual units;

- In which 33% of all units are owner occupied or second homes;

- In which 60% of the units in the building are sold or under contract.

Ineligible Property for a non-recourse loan according to the North American Savings Bank program includes:

- Residential with large acreage

- Raw land

- Farms

- Manufactured or log homes

- Nonwarrantable condos (includes most condo conversions and those less than 100% complete)

- Hotels, condo-hotels, short-term rentals

- Co-ops, timeshares

- Senior- or assisted-living facilities

- Nonfranchise restaurants

- Entertainment properties

- Mini-storage

Purchasing a property

In order to obtain a non-recourse loan within your IRA, North American Savings Bank will need to verify the amount of IRA assets available for purchase along with minimal reserves equal to 10% to 20% of the loan amount, depending on certain criteria. Since the IRA is providing the money for the transaction, there is no employment or income verification necessary for the account owner.

Because these properties are investment properties and they alone secure the non-recourse loan, there are some income requirements for the rental properties. The financed property must generate sufficient net operating income (NOI) to exceed the debt service payments. Single-family homes must generate a 20% to 25% positive cash flow with sufficient reserves. Properties that have two to four units should have a NOI of 25% or more positive cash flow.

Example

Let's assume Michael has worked for a large corporation for 30 years and has accumulated $400,000 in his 401(k) plan offered by his employer. He finally made the decision to retire and wants to rollover his 401(k) plan into a self-directed IRA. He's talked to two or three self-directed IRA custodians and decided that real estate is a good investment option for his retirement plan.

Michael is an avid golfer who belongs to a country club in his hometown. He noticed a single-family home for sale on his golf course and he thinks it would be a good rental. Michael plays golf on this course three or four days a week, which will allow him to keep an eye on his investment. What should Michael do next?

Steps to purchasing property

While talking to a self-directed custodian, Michael learns that he can leverage investment real estate with a non-recourse loan. The custodian recommends Michael call a non-recourse lender to prequalify the property. He really likes the thought of using debt financing to purchase this single-family home so he can limit the investment from his IRA to 50% of the purchase price which will allow Michael to purchase more rental property and invest in other asset classes.

Michael contacts North American Savings Bank, who asks him to gather some basic information on the property. North American Savings Bank offers to prequalify the property before Michael makes his offer. The following information is required to prequalify a property for a non-recourse loan.

Type of property _____

(e.g., single-family home, condo, duplex, multifamily)

Purchase price _____

Estimated value _____

Address _____

City and State _____

Current liquid balances in all retirement accounts (IRA, 401(k), etc.)

_____

Has the property sold in the last three years? Yes No

If yes, the date of sale and price? _____

Is this new construction? Yes No

Livable square footage _____

Year property was built _____

Estimated monthly rental income _____

Is there an annual lease in place? Yes No, Amount? $_____

Will there be an annual lease in place before closing? Yes No

Will you use a property manager? Yes No

Taxes _____ Insurance _____

HOA dues (if applicable) _____

If property needs repairs, please list _____

Digital picture or web link to the property

If a refinance:

Original purchase price _____

Original purchase date _____

Have you made any improvements to the property? Yes No

If yes, how much did you spend on improvements? _____

Do you have a lien on the property? Yes No

If yes, what is the current loan balance? _____

NASB analyzes Michael's property and calculates its cash flow numbers to determine the debt service coverage ratio (DSCR). Below is a breakdown of the DSCR for Michael's $200,000 purchase. This will give Michael a good indication of what to expect if he collects the $1,400/month rent he anticipates the property to generate.

Debt Service Coverage Ratio Example
$200,000 property (single-family home) with a $100,000 IRA non-recourse loan

Gross Annual Income (GAI):	
Rent	$16,800
($1,400/month × 12)	
Costs:	
Vacancy (7% × GAI)	$-1,176
Real Estate Taxes	$-2,500
Property Casualty Insurance	$-800
Maintenance ($420/unit)	$-420
Management Fee (6% × GAI)	$-1,008
Net Operating Income (NOI)	**$10,896**

Michael should expect a NOI of $10,896 based on the above estimated costs. NASB uses a 7% vacancy factor, $420 in annual anticipated maintenance/repairs and 6% for a management fee. These three variables are estimates and may differ depending on the specific real estate market. Let's take a closer look at this scenario when we factor in the $100,000 non-recourse loan. The lender currently offers a 25-year fixed loan at a 7% interest rate.

The annual principal and interest is $8,482, based on a $100,000 loan at 7% with a 25-year amortization.

Formula for Debt Service Coverage Ratio

Net Operating Income/Annual Principal and Interest = Debt Service Coverage Ratio

$$\$10,896/\$8,482 = 1.28 \text{ DSCR}$$

In this example, the annualized net operating income exceeds the mortgage payments (principal and interest) by 28%, or the net operating income is 1.28 times the debt service payments. The breakeven is 1.0, and anything above 1.0 is positive cash flow. The cash flow goes back into the IRA to grow tax-free or tax-deferred.

The lender tells Michael that this property qualifies based on the information provided and offers him a non-recourse loan preapproval letter to provide with his offer to the seller. Michael makes an offer on the property for $200,000, and the seller accepts.

First steps

The first step to investing in real estate with your IRA funds is to set up a self-directed IRA. You must choose an IRA custodian or administrator who is familiar with and allows real estate investments within an IRA. All transactions must be handled by the custodian or administrator in order to meet the rules set out by the IRS. A list of self-directed IRA custodians/administrators and other self-directed companies is provided in the back of this book and also at www.iralending.com.

Back to our example: Michael chooses ABC Trust Company to administer his self-directed IRA. He rolls over his $400,000 401(k) to ABC Trust Company and is ready to move forward with the purchase.

Note: The buyer's name on the purchase contract must be the IRA. In this example the buyer is "ABC Trust Company, Custodian FBO (First Name Last Name), IRA". The real estate contract, title work, and insurance all need to be in the name of the IRA and not your personal name. FBO stands for "for the benefit of".

Below is a list of items Michael will provide to the lender for the transaction:

- Loan application/checklist of items.

- Most recent IRA statement verifying IRA assets for purchase and reserves.

- Real estate sales contract titled correctly in the name of the IRA or other entity.

- Copy of the account holders driver's license.

- Direction of Investment form completed for the IRA custodian.

- Property casualty insurance policy.

- Appraisal fee so lender can order the real estate appraisal. The appraisal fee must be paid by the IRA.

A non-recourse lender will order a full-investment property appraisal to verify the current market value of the property and to provide rent comparables to verify the current market rents in the area. This is the most important variable when a lender is underwriting the loan. An appraisal helps the lender determine if the property is valued correctly. A lender will not offer a final approval until after a bank underwriter reviews the appraisal and concurs the collateral is sufficient to secure the loan.

Non-recourse loans normally average 30 days to close from the date the appraisal was ordered. Let's assume Michael is buying this single-family home in Missouri and ABC Trust Company is in Texas. The lender will forward the closing documents to the title company in Missouri; Michael will "read and approve" all the documents and deliver them to ABC Trust Company in Texas by overnight delivery. ABC Trust Company will execute the documents (this is the signature required before the loan can be funded) and return the executed loan documents to the title company in Missouri. The loan will be funded once the title company receives the closing documents from the IRA custodian. It's recommended that you allow yourself an extra three to five days for the closing process due to the shipping of documents between the lender, IRA account holder, and the IRA custodian/administrator.

After the loan closes, the IRA is responsible for making the monthly mortgage payments to the lender. The IRA custodian/administrator will disburse funds from the IRA account that owns the real estate and mail the checks to the lender and all rental income is deposited directly into the IRA account once it is received from the tenant. All the property management costs will come out of the IRA such as real estate taxes, property casualty insurance, and repairs. A non-recourse lender will normally escrow for real estate taxes and property casualty insurance, paying them when they are due.

Michael closes on the loan and is very happy with his new investment. This is a scenario played out thousands of times as investors learn that real estate investing within an IRA can be profitable while providing diversification. It can also be an avenue for investment for those who may not qualify personally for an investment mortgage as the normal requirements of income and credit score do not apply. Although there are IRS rules to understand, there are many qualified specialists and professionals to help you with every stop of the way.

CHAPTER 5

The Unrelated Business Income Tax and Your IRA

Eric Wikstrom, CPA, CFP®

In chapter 3, we touched briefly on how you need to understand the two pools of capital that you can draw from: your taxable pocket and your tax-advantaged pocket. We also briefly looked at why it may—yes, *may*—make sense to make an investment in your IRA and actually pay tax out of your IRA versus making the investment with your taxable pocket and paying substantially more tax.

In this chapter, we are going to look deeper at the inner workings of the unrelated business income tax (UBIT) as it relates to IRAs. I think you'll find that, as the officials in the National Football League would tell you "upon further review," the entire issue around an IRA investing in leveraged real estate is usually a nonissue.

What is UBIT and what is its purpose?

The UBIT was injected by Congress into the Internal Revenue Code (IRC) in the 1950 Revenue Act. Its basic purpose was to level the playing field between tax-exempt entities like churches, charities, and universities that operated a trade or business versus their tax-paying competitors that were not tax-exempt owner entities.

This came into play with tax-exempt entities that either owned or inherited a fully-functioning business. Groups like churches and universities would inherit an ongoing, long-time operating, profitable business from one of their parishioners or alumni, and, because these tax-exempt entities met the qualifications under IRC section 501(c)(3), they would pay no federal income tax on their operations. But it became apparent to Congress that there were too many situations where these tax-exempt entities were operating these profitable businesses and paying no income tax. It was obvious that these groups had an unfair advantage over their tax-paying competitors that were owned by others who ultimately did pay federal income tax on their net income.

Along came the UBIT. When IRAs were created in 1974 by a tax act known as ERISA, they ultimately got thrown into the UBIT net because they too are tax-exempt entities. There are really only two areas that you need to be concerned about related to IRAs: (1) if your IRA is an owner or investor in a trade or business or (2) if your IRA uses debt in the acquisition of real estate.

Your IRA, a trade or business, and UBIT

The first area where the UBIT might affect your IRA is if your IRA makes an investment in an ongoing trade or business. Now you might be thinking, "I own 100 shares of Microsoft in my IRA and the last time I checked, Microsoft was operating a trade or business. Does my IRA have to pay UBIT because I own 100 shares of Microsoft?" The answer is no and that is because the UBIT does not apply if an investment by an IRA is made in a publicly traded entity, because a publicly traded entity by nature must be a C corporation, which pays federal income tax on its net taxable income. The IRA is not subjected to "double taxation" by paying UBIT again.

Remember, the only three investments your IRA can't own are: (1) collectibles, (2) life insurance, and (3) S-corporation stock. It is perfectly acceptable for your IRA to own all of or part of a fast-food franchise, for example. To equalize the tax-playing field, the income from the fast- food franchise would be subject to income tax (in this case the UBIT) just like your competitor across the street, even if the fast-food franchise is owned entirely by a tax-exempt entity like your IRA.

Your IRA, debt with real estate, and UBIT

When Congress created the concept of UBIT, they were kind enough to exclude rents from real estate from UBIT taxation. However, they also decided that a real estate activity financed with debt would be subject to tax, but only to *the portion of the income that was debt financed*. That is the important factor here. If a loan of 50% of the purchase price was used to buy real property, then only 50% of the income from the property would be subject to the UBIT. That's not a bad deal, really.

Why is this not a bad deal? Because, as we'll soon find out, if you make an investment in real estate that produces taxable income, chances are you'll pay much more in regular federal income tax than you would pay in UBIT!

How the UBIT is calculated

The actual calculation behind the UBIT is quite simple. If you can multiply a fraction by a whole number, you've conquered UBIT!

The UBIT ingredients:

1. **The amount of debt used to purchase the real estate**

2. **The cost of the real estate**

3. **The net taxable income the property generates**

That's it. Let's take a look at how we assemble the three pieces for our UBIT calculation.

Before we get started, let's make some assumptions for our example.

Date of real estate purchase:	7/1/201x
Cost of real estate purchase:	$510,000
Beginning loan on real estate at purchase:	$300,000

The debt piece

The first step is to determine what the *average acquisition indebtedness* is for the part of the tax year the IRA holds the property. This is computed by taking the principal outstanding on the first day of each calendar month, adding these amounts, and dividing the sum by the number of months the property is held. This average debt amount forms the numerator in our UBIT calculation. In our example below, the average acquisition indebtedness is $250,000.

Month	Month #	Principal Balance at beginning of each month
July	1	$300,000
August	2	$280,000
September	3	$260,000
October	4	$240,000
November	5	$220,000
December	6	$200,000
		$1,500,000

Average Acquisition Indebtedness Calculation:

Total Principal Balance on first day of each month	$1,500,000
Divided by # of months loan outstanding during year	6
= Average Acquisition Indebtedness	$250,000

The cost piece

This is the cost "basis" of the property as of the first and last day that the IRA holds the property during the tax year. The most common adjustment is for depreciation. The average cost basis forms the denominator of our UBIT calculation. From the calculation below, the average cost basis for year one is $500,000.

Purchase Price of Real Estate 7/1/201x	$510,000
Less: Depreciation for period ending 12/31/201x	-$20,000
Cost basis as of 12/31/201x	$490,000
Average Cost basis calculation:	
Beginning period cost basis	$510,000
Ending period cost basis	$490,000
Total	$1,000,000
Divisor for average calculation	2
Average Cost basis:	$500,000

The net income piece

The third piece of the UBIT calculation is very simple and that is the computation of the taxable net income from the real estate. This calculation method is exactly the same as if you had owned real estate with your taxable funds and had reported the result on Schedule E. Because many CPAs and financial planners are not familiar with the actual mechanics involved with the calculation, they erroneously assume that you "lose" depreciation with real estate in your IRA. This is not the case at all as you can see from the calculation below.

Rents		$64,000
Less expenses:		
Depreciation	$20,000	
Interest expense	$10,000	
Insurance	$4,000	
Real Estate Taxes	$12,000	
Repairs	$6,500	
Misc.	$1,500	$54,000
Gross Income from Debt Financed Property		$10,000

Now let's put the three pieces together:

$$\frac{\text{Average Acquisition Indebtedness}}{\text{Average Cost Basis}} \times \quad \text{Gross Income from Debt Financed Property}$$

$$= \frac{\$250,000}{\$500,000} \times \$10,000$$

$$= 50\% \times \$10,000$$

$$= \text{Unrelated Debt Financed Income} = \$5,000$$

After we've crunched the numbers, you'll see that we'll pay some tax out of our IRA. This is because we have positive taxable income and hence, positive UBIT.

However, before you get too alarmed with paying tax out of your IRA, let's see how much it will be and compare it to the tax you would pay if you had owned this real estate investment *outside* your IRA.

Tax on Annual Operations:	Real Estate Investment held in IRA	Real Estate Investment held outside IRA
Regular Taxable Income	N/A	$10,000
Gross Income from Debt Financed property	$10,000	N/A
Debt % applied to Income	50%	N/A
Income before special deduction	$5,000	$10,000
Specific UBTI Deduction	$1,000	N/A
Taxable Income	$4,000	$10,000
Applicable Tax Rate	20%	20%
Income Tax	$800	$2,000

What's the moral to the story with UBIT? Because the UBIT calculation includes a reduction to gross income based on the percentage of debt financing each year, and the fact that you get a $1,000 UBIT deduction, the amount taxed for UBIT purposes is *usually* substantially less than the amount taxed for regular income tax purposes if you had owned the same investment with your taxable funds.

Is the UBIT the big bad bogeyman that you had been led to believe by other professionals? As the examples above show, the UBIT tax usually isn't that painful. Make good, sound real estate investments, and if you have to pay some UBIT, rest assured that it is usually less than you'd pay from your taxable pocket.

CHAPTER 6

How the UBIT Effects Operations and Sales

Eric Wikstrom, CPA, CFP®

In the last chapter, we introduced the concept of the unrelated business income tax (UBIT), when and why it applied, and how it was calculated on an annual basis on leveraged real estate owned by your IRA. Even though most real estate is purchased with the thought that it probably will be held for longer periods of time than most traditional stock market-type investments, it is important to understand what effect UBIT plays not only on the annual operations of your real estate investment, but on the sale of real estate when it ultimately occurs.

In this chapter, we'll walk through two examples to make sure you are crystal clear on what the UBIT issues are during the ownership period as well as on the sale of real estate within your IRA.

Our two examples are based on a situation that is very common in utilizing an IRA to invest in real estate: the purchase of a single-family residential rental property. The only difference between our two scenarios is the amount of monthly rental income. For the first example, the rental property receives rents of $3,000 per month versus $2,250 per month in the second example. The purpose for showing different monthly rental income is to highlight the situation over a period of years where a property consistently has positive taxable income subject to UBIT versus a situation (and very common in early rental real estate operations) where the net taxable rental income subject to UBIT is actually a loss.

(Author's note: to make the examples as easy to understand as possible, some slight rounding of calculations has been made.)

We'll demonstrate how in example one the annual taxable losses are carried forward until the date of sale in year five versus example two where, because of positive taxable income, the taxes are paid annually from the IRA.

The following is the general data, information, and assumptions for our case studies:

Type	Single Family	Single Family
Purchase date	1/1/2010	1/1/2010
Sale date	12/31/2014	12/31/2014
Purchase amount	$365,000	$365,000
Amount of purchase allocated to land	25%	25%
Amount available for depreciation	$275,000	$275,000
Depreciation term and method	27.5 years/ Straight line	27.5 years/ Straight line
Financial Information	**Example #1**	**Example #2**
Down payment	$182,500	$182,500
% of purchase price	50%	50%
Loan amount	$182,500	$182,500
Interest rate	7.0%	7.0%
Term (years)	30	30
Monthly principal & interest	$1,214	$1,214
INCOME & EXPENSES	**Example #1**	**Example #2**
Monthly rents	$2,250	$3,000
Annual rents	$27,000	$36,000
Annual operating expenses	$11,250	$11,250
Annual debt service (P&I)	$14,570	$14,570

ASSUMPTIONS	Example #1	Example #2
Rental growth rate	2%	2%
Expense growth rate	2%	2%
Property appreciation rate	2%	2%
Future selling expenses as % of sales price	6%	6%

Example 1:

Let's take a look at the annual operating property data for example one based on the assumptions outlined above.

Example 1: Rental Activity & Tax Analysis: Table 1A

RENTAL ACTIVITY	ITEM #	YEAR 1 2010	YEAR 2 2011	YEAR 3 2012	YEAR 4 2013	YEAR 5 2014
Annual rental income	1	$ 27,000	$ 27,540	$ 28,091	$ 28,653	$ 29,226
Less: Operating expenses	2	$ (11,250)	$ (11,475)	$ (11,705)	$ (11,939)	$ (12,177)
Net Operating Income	3	$ 15,750	$ 16,065	$ 16,386	$ 16,714	$ 17,048
Less: Tax Depreciation	4	$ (9,583)	$ (10,000)	$ (10,000)	$ (10,000)	$ (10,000)
Less: Interest Expense	5	$ (11,662)	$ (12,594)	$ (12,451)	$ (12,298)	$ (12,133)
Taxable Income	6	$ (5,495)	$ (6,529)	$ (6,065)	$ (5,584)	$ (5,085)
Unrelated Debt-Financed Income (UDFI) %	7	50.41%	51.27%	52.17%	53.08%	54.00%
Unrelated Debt-Financed Income - (UDFI)	8	$ (2,770)	$ (3,347)	$ (3,164)	$ (2,964)	$ (2,746)
Net Operating Loss Deduction - (NOL)	9	N/A	$ (2,770)	$ (6,117)	$ (9,281)	$ (12,245)
Unrelated Business Taxable Income - (UBTI)	10	$ (2,770)	$ (6,117)	$ (9,281)	$ (12,245)	$ (14,991)
CASH FLOW ANALYSIS	ITEM #	YEAR 1 2010	YEAR 2 2011	YEAR 3 2012	YEAR 4 2013	YEAR 5 2014
Net Operating Income (from above)	11	$ 15,750	$ 16,065	$ 16,386	$ 16,714	$ 17,048
Less: Annual debt service	12	$ (14,570)	$ (14,570)	$ (14,570)	$ (14,570)	$ (14,570)
Cash Flow before Taxes	13	$ 1,180	$ 1,495	$ 1,816	$ 2,144	$ 2,478
UBIT Expense	14	$ 0	$ 0	$ 0	$ 0	$ 0
Cash Flow after Taxes	15	$ 1,180	$ 1,495	$ 1,816	$ 2,144	$ 2,478

Analysis of example 1

A quick review of example one points out a very common situation for owners of real estate, whether it be residential, commercial, or industrial property: regardless of property size and rental income, it is very common for property (especially in the early years) to generate zero or very little positive *cash flow* and at the same time generate *substantial tax losses*. Why does this happen? The main reason is depreciation. You see, depreciation is a *noncash deduction* for income tax purposes and, because there is no cash outflow, depreciation has no effect at all on any cash flow analysis.

For purposes of calculating taxable income for unrelated business income tax purposes, depreciation *is actually taken into account* (see line item number four on the previous page). This method of calculating taxable income for UBIT purposes *is exactly the same* as if you owned property outside your IRA with your taxable funds (in that case, the rental investment computation would go on Schedule E, then on to your Form 1040).

However, before we move on, let's examine the difference between our cash flow before taxes (line item number 13) and the taxable income number (line item number six). The only differences are depreciation (included in the taxable income result but not cash flow) and debt service and interest expense (debt service is principal and interest), are included in the cash flow result, whereas only interest is deductible for tax purposes.

In years one through five, the annual operating activity for the property will generate negative taxable income and positive cash flow. This is the best of all worlds! Because cash flow is what we stick in our pocket (or what goes back into the IRA in this case), and taxable income (whether it is calculated for UBIT or regular tax purposes) is what we use to determine how much in tax we'll pay to the government.

UBIT and net operating losses

Knowing what we know now, a quick glance at all the years of taxable income (line item number six) tells us that because we don't have any year with positive taxable income; our IRA will not owe any UBIT at all. But what about the negative taxable income numbers? Do we get any benefit from having taxable losses in prior years? Yes, we do! We get the same benefit for UBIT purposes that we do for regular tax purposes as it relates to tax loss carry forwards.

Let's examine what happens to our negative taxable income for year 2010. Year 2010 generated a taxable loss of ($5,495) (see line item number six for year 2010). But for UBIT purposes, we must multiply the taxable income result, positive or negative, by the debt/cost basis ratio that we discussed in our previous chapter. At the end of year 2010, the average debt to average cost basis ratio was 50.41% (see line item number seven, year 2010). This 50.41% is multiplied by the negative taxable income of ($5,495) to give a net operating loss carry forward of ($2,770) to year 2011 (see line item number nine, year 2011).

This process of carrying forward the taxable losses continues until we have a year with positive taxable income. At that point, we could utilize as much of the tax loss carry forwards as are available to offset any positive taxable income for that year. If the tax loss carry forwards were fully utilized in a single year, then most likely some UBIT tax would be due. However, if the taxable income in a future year was not enough to fully offset the loss carry forwards, these losses could continue to be carried forward into the future.

UBIT on sale of the property

Up to this point, we've been focused on UBIT and its effect (if any) on annual property operations. We've seen in example one that, because of negative taxable income, this property has generated net operating losses that can be used to offset future positive income. However, what about when we sell the property with net operating losses that we haven't been able to utilize fully, or even at all?

Let's see how we utilize the net operating loss carry forwards with the sale of the property at the end of year five.

Example 1: Property Sale Analysis - Table 1B

TAX ANALYSIS - PROPERTY SALE	ITEM #	YEAR 5 12/31/2014
Adjusted Projected Sales Price (2% appreciation)	1	$ 402,989
Less: Selling expenses (6% of sales price)	2	$ (24,179)
Net Sales Price (Amount realized)	3	$ 378,810
Original cost of property	4	$ 365,000
Less: accumulated depreciation	5	$ (49,583)
Adjusted basis of property	6	$ 315,417
Taxable Gain/(Loss) on sale of property (item #3 - item #6)	7	$ 63,393
Unrelated Debt-Financed Income (UDFI) %	8	54.38%
Unrelated Debt-Financed Income	9	$ 34,473
Net Operating Loss Deduction Carryforward (NOL)	10	$ (14,991)
UBIT deduction	11	$ (1,000)
Unrelated Business Taxable Income (UBTI)	12	$ 18,483
UBIT tax at capital gain rate (15%)	13	$ 2,772

Analysis from the sale of example one property

Before we get too deep in the analysis on the sale of the property in year five, let's make note of a couple important items:

When the real estate owned by an IRA is sold and the property is still encumbered by debt at the time of the sale, the debt/cost basis ratio to use in the sale analysis is *the average monthly ratio over the past twelve months from the date of the sale.* For purposes of this sale calculation, the highest debt/cost ratio was 54.38% (see line item number eight). *If debt is paid off 12 months before the sale date of the property, there is no capital gain tax owed at all on the sale of the property.*

The reason that the debt/cost basis ratio at the time of sale in year five (see line item number eight) 54.38% is greater than it was at inception five years ago, 50%, is that the numerator in this calculation, the loan, is being amortized over 30 years versus 75% of the property value being depreciated over 27.5 years. Therefore, the ratio is actually increasing slightly each year. If extra principal payments were being made (in this example, they are not), the ratio most likely would decrease over time.

For purposes of calculation simplicity, a 15% capital gain tax was used for this UBIT analysis. A tax law change in 1997 provides for a maximum 25% rate on long-term capital gains attributable to "unrecaptured section 1250 gain." At lower income levels like this example, the total capital gain tax is usually closer to 15%.

Conclusions

What are the important items to note from the sale analysis? Up to line item number seven, the sale calculation for UBIT is exactly the same as for regular tax purposes. At line item number eight, we use the debt/cost basis ratio to reduce the amount of capital gain subject to UBIT taxation. However, before we make the capital gain calculation, we need to determine what our net operating loss carry forwards are, taking into account the activity for the year of sale.

We saw from the annual taxable income calculation above in Table 1A, line item number ten that our net operating loss carry forward at the end of year five was $14,991. Fortunately, when the property is sold, we get to utilize any unused net operating loss against the sale of the property. So the unrelated debt-financed income (UDFI) capital gain (see line item number nine) gets reduced by this amount of net operating loss. This, along with the standard $1,000 UBIT deduction, reduces the UBIT subject to capital gain tax to $18,483. This is the amount taxed at capital gain rates, which generates a capital gain tax of $2,772, payable from the IRA account.

Example 2: Rental Activity & Tax Analysis - Table 2A

RENTAL ACTIVITY	ITEM #	YEAR 1 2010	YEAR 2 2011	YEAR 3 2012	YEAR 4 2013	YEAR 5 2014
Annual rental income	1	$ 36,000	$ 36,720	$ 37,454	$ 38,203	$ 38,968
Less: Operating expenses	2	$ (11,250)	$ (11,475)	$ (11,705)	$ (11,939)	$ (12,177)
Net Operating Income	3	$ 24,750	$ 25,245	$ 25,749	$ 26,264	$ 26,791
Less: Tax Depreciation	4	$ (9,583)	$ (10,000)	$ (10,000)	$ (10,000)	$ (10,000)
Less: Interest Expense	5	$ (11,662)	$ (12,594)	$ (12,451)	$ (12,298)	$ (12,133)
Taxable Income	6	$ 3,505	$ 2,651	$ 3,298	$ 3,966	$ 4,658
Unrelated Debt-Financed Income (UDFI) %	7	50.41%	51.27%	52.17%	53.08%	54.00%
Unrelated Debt-Financed Income - (UDFI)	8	$ 1,767	$ 1,359	$ 1,721	$ 2,105	$ 2,515
UBIT Deduction	9	$ (1,000)	$ (1,000)	$ (1,000)	$ (1,000)	$ (1,000)
Unrelated Business Taxable Income - (UBTI)	10	$ 767	$ 359	$ 721	$ 1,105	$ 1,515
UBIT Tax due	11	$ 115	$ 54	$ 108	$ 166	$ 227
CASH FLOW ANALYSIS	ITEM #	YEAR 1 2010	YEAR 2 2011	YEAR 3 2012	YEAR 4 2013	YEAR 5 2014
Net Operating Income (from above)	12	$ 24,750	$ 25,245	$ 25,749	$ 26,264	$ 26,791
Less: Annual debt service	13	$ (14,570)	$ (14,570)	$ (14,570)	$ (14,570)	$ (14,570)
Cash Flow before Taxes	14	$ 10,180	$ 10,675	$ 11,179	$ 11,694	$ 12,221
UBIT Expense	15	$ 115	$ 54	$ 108	$ 166	$ 227
Cash Flow after Taxes	16	$ 10,065	$ 10,621	$ 11,071	$ 11,528	$ 11,994

Analysis of example two

The main difference between examples one and two is that example two has greater rental income (see line item number one in Table 2A) and hence positive taxable income from inception of property operations (see line item number six).

After taxable income is calculated, the appropriate debt/cost basis ratio is applied to the taxable income number each year (see line item number seven). After the UDFI is calculated, we apply the $1,000 standard deduction to arrive at the UBTI number subject to tax at trust tax rates (see lines items 10 and 11).

Because years one through five all have positive UBTI after the $1,000 standard deduction, tax is due by April 15 of the following year. If taxable income becomes negative for any year, that net operating loss can be carried back three years and applied to UBIT previously paid, or the loss can be carried forward to offset any future UBIT that will be owed.

A key point to note here is that any UBIT tax due is to be paid out of the IRA account as opposed to payment from the IRA accountholder's personal funds. Proper planning is important so that the IRA account has enough liquid funds to pay the UBIT tax due. Unfortunately, the IRA account does not get any credit or tax basis for any UBIT tax liability paid.

As we noted earlier, the method of "keeping score" for UBIT taxable income is different than for cash flow analysis. But as you can tell from line items numbers 15 and 16, because UBIT tax paid is actually a cash outflow, UBIT taxes should be recognized in any financial analysis that is concerned with net after-tax cash flows.

Example 2: Property Sale Analysis - Table 2B

TAX ANALYSIS - PROPERTY SALE	ITEM #	YEAR 5 12/31/2014
Adjusted Projected Sales Price (2% appreciation)	1	$ 402,989
Less: Selling expenses (6% of sales price)	2	$ (24,179)
Net Sales Price (Amount realized)	3	$ 378,810
Original cost of property	4	$ 365,000
Less: accumulated depreciation	5	$ (49,583)
Adjusted basis of property	6	$ 315,417
Taxable Gain/(Loss) on sale of property (item #3 - item #6)	7	$ 63,393
Unrelated Debt-Financed Income (UDFI) %	8	54.38%
Unrelated Debt-Financed Income	9	$ 34,473
UBIT tax owing at capital gain rate (15%)	12	$ 5,170

UBIT on sale of the property

Because example two does not have any tax loss carry forwards, the capital gain calculation on the sale of the property at the end of year five is simpler than it was in example one. The calculation of gain or loss in Table 2B up to line item number seven is the same regardless of whether you are making this calculation for an IRA account or with regular taxable funds.

But because the IRA only has to pay capital gain tax on the portion of the gain that is debt financed (the average monthly ratio of debt to cost basis), we need to multiply the capital gain determined on line item number seven by the debt to cost basis ratio on line number eight to arrive at net UDFI subject to tax at capital gains rates.

Overall conclusions

The general methodology used in calculating UBIT is really no different than calculating annual rental taxable income or gain/loss on the sale of rental property. The main difference is that in the UBIT world, you reduce the amount of taxable income by the debt to cost basis ratio before you apply the trust tax rate (IRAs are treated as trusts under UBIT rules; thus, the trust tax rate applies). As you can see from the examples in the tables above, the debt-to-cost basis ratio changes every year due to debt service payments (numerator) and depreciation (denominator).

In cases where the taxable income is negative (very common in real estate investments due to the depreciation deduction), there will be no UBIT due on annual property operations. This can result in net operating loss carry backs and carry forwards of prior and future UBIT.

Even though the UBIT concept is geared toward "tax-exempt" entities, all common items like the net operating loss, capital gains and losses, depreciation, etc., retain their "usual" tax treatment. The common belief that IRAs shouldn't invest in real estate because they "lose tax benefits" doesn't exactly hold water. Although rents are exempt from UBIT, when an IRA leverages real estate, items like depreciation, interest, property taxes, etc., do become useful and meaningful for reduction of the IRA's tax obligation.

CHAPTER 7

Finding Properties

For those investors who want something other than the standard portfolio of stocks and bonds, real estate investing can provide a tangible asset that the investor can actually see rather than a generic quarterly statement. Many people enjoy the search for and management of properties, and using these real estate-related skills to enhance the returns from their IRA is an additional bonus. However, experience in real estate investing isn't required. While it may seem a little daunting at first, finding the right real estate investments just requires some research and awareness of what is around you every day. You can begin with a single property.

It is important to understand how to analyze your local real estate market and discover which neighborhoods and subdivisions may offer investment potential suitable for your purposes. If you are using debt financing by way of an IRA non-recourse loan, then you must also take into consideration the types of properties that are open for consideration for available non-recourse loan programs as well as the cash flow required to service the debt and pay operating expenses, including any UBIT that may apply.

One of the first questions that beginning real estate investors should ask is where they should invest. It is usually beneficial to purchase your first few investment properties close to your current location. It will be easier to monitor them, and you will have peace of mind if you can occasionally drive by your investment. Once you become an experienced real estate investor, you can start considering more distant opportunities.

The first bit of research that you will want to undertake is looking at your regional economy. Determine if the market is improving and its rate of housing unit growth. Who are the major employers and are they likely to add jobs locally? What kinds of jobs and levels of employment are they providing? Are the jobs high-paying professional positions or middle income factory positions? Most of this information can be obtained from your local chamber of commerce or your local public library. You can also find information on occupancy rates, population density, and a host of other wage and occupation information from the Bureau of Labor statistics (www.bls.com).

This research will give you a snapshot look at the specific market where you intend to invest. If your area is very depressed economically, you may want to consider another area that is stable or experiencing some growth and has more potential. A good measure of the rental market in any area is the occupancy rate of apartment complexes. If there is a large number of unoccupied rental units available in your area, you must consider the impact these vacant units will have on your ability to find a tenant quickly and at a monthly rental rate sufficient to provide cash flow. A high vacancy rate in your market may affect the rates you can charge tenants or result in a prolonged vacancy. Also, you will want to educate yourself about the number of pending foreclosures and the number of foreclosures (bank owned) listings in your preferred area. Banks are not in the business to hold real estate. They will reduce their prices until the properties sell fairly quickly. An over abundance of foreclosure real estate, or foreclosures in process may indicate the area could experience further declines in the market values. Excess housing inventory could also create excess rental property inventory which can hurt your projected lease (rents) rates.

Once you have chosen a promising location to invest, you will want to research the area in more detail. There are several factors that will determine which neighborhoods, or even which blocks within that neighborhood, should be considered.

1. Schools—If you don't have school age children this may not be a major concern at first, but it should be. Remember that you are entering the rental market and many young families with children are renters. Schools and their ranking within the community are a

determining factor for parents when they choose where to live. Most will pay more for housing in a great school district, and renters with children typically occupy a property longer than the average renter, a good school is a key consideration. Choosing a property in a good school district is an opportunity to be in an area where it is easier to attract long-term renters and thus lower vacancy rates. Most schools have their own website where their scores and student rankings are listed in comparison to local and national averages. You may also want to talk to a good realtor who is familiar with the area who can quickly tell you which areas are the most in demand for families with school age children.

2. University areas—The area and neighborhoods around universities or local colleges are good locations in which to acquire rental property. The homes surrounding these schools are usually well kept, and many of the students and professionals who work at the university require housing within walking distance.

3. Percentage of owner-occupied properties—It is a well-known fact that owner-occupied dwellings are better maintained than rentals. Many people refer to this as pride of ownership. It is a relatively simple matter to drive through a neighborhood you are considering to guesstimate how many homes are owner occupied. How many have yards that are well kept? Do the homes look well maintained? Does the community have a good home owners association? Are the vacant lots free of clutter? This can give you a general indication as to whether or not the homes in the neighborhood are owner occupied which increases the value for potential renters. Nobody wants to live in an area that is in a declining condition, where trash and overgrown yards are the norm. They want a community—a place that looks like home. This is important to remember when looking for properties. A property that looks like a steal may not be if the property sits in a declining area of town where very few homes are owner occupied. Sometimes, it is better to pay a little more for an investment property if the house is located in a great area of town, even if it needs a little work. The long-term cash flow prospects for this property can be good, and the resale prospects and appreciation may be much better.

4. Safety—This is an important consideration for most people who are looking for housing. Everybody wants to feel as if they are living in a safe environment. You can easily find crime statistics for any neighborhood, and there are also sex offender databases that are maintained by local law enforcement. Clusters of crime or sex offenders in a particular area indicate an environment that may be unsafe and will hinder your ability to attract renters.

5. Big business—Look in the immediate area where you are planning to invest as well as the areas in close proximity for major employers. The cost of commuting is skyrocketing for everyone and has become a major factor when considering housing options. It is also important to understand that, unless the employer is a governmental entity, there is always a chance that a single company could perform poorly and downsize. Should that one large employer fold, it would shrink the pool of renters—and it may also have a detrimental effect on the area's total housing market, making it difficult to sell the property in the future. There are good opportunities in areas surrounding large employers, as long as you understand the risk.

6. Malls and shopping centers—Distance to shopping, dining, and entertainment are important factors. When you drive through a neighborhood you are considering for investment, take note of how close the area is to these retail areas, including grocery stores. If the retailers are moving to another area of town and there are vacant stores, you might want to reconsider your investment in that area.

7. Public transportation—Transportation in urban areas is an important feature. Close proximity to a train line and bus route will have appeal to many city dwellers.

Assessing value

Professional appraisers are hired by the lender to give an opinion of value for the real estate. Often, an investor can become upset if the appraisal is lower than expected. In reality, appraisers are doing their job by offering an unbiased opinion of market value. If the appraised value is lower than expected, the lower value should be used to renegotiate your purchase price with the seller. After all, you want to avoid overpaying for your investment. They know something that you don't know. Remember, lenders are in the business of lending money. They want to give you a loan, but only if the loan is secured with sufficient collateral and equity.

Many investors start their real estate investing by purchasing fixer-uppers. They will repair these properties and quickly sell (flip) them or use them as rental property. This allows investors to stretch their cash even further by getting a very good price on the initial purchase and then renting the property at a much higher rate when the repairs are complete, thus increasing the possible cash flow. If you plan to purchase property in need of repairs or major rehab, be sure to obtain complete work estimates from at least two licensed contractors prior to making a purchase offer. Remember that all repairs must be paid by your IRA.

For those who choose to pursue this distressed-property market, it is good to bring along an experienced mentor who can point out opportunities for greater gains as well as steer you away from properties that may turn into a money pit. Since there are so many investors who specialize in this market, many qualified realtors will be able to give you some names or introductions to other investors or experts who can help you.

When looking for a distressed property that will offer substantial gain you must consider the following:

1. Location is everything—The whole idea of fixing up properties for resale is to acquire the biggest net increase in property value. Looking for the worst homes in the best neighborhoods may present the best opportunities. If you try to buy distressed property in a declining part of town, you run the risk of putting more into the property than it will ever be worth and not being able to rent the property at acceptable rates. Having said this, you can make nearly any property work for you if you purchase at the right price and keep your costs low by not spending too much for property repairs and rehab.

2. Cosmetic fixes—Properties in need of cosmetic work are the easiest and fastest to prepare for renters. These properties are generally sound from a structural point of view and have good plumbing and electrical

systems. If you spend a relatively small amount of money to replace flooring, upgrade light fixtures and appliances, and do some painting and landscaping, you will improve the property value while reducing the time to lease the property, and the appeal to prospective tenants. You should also be able to command top rents for your market.

3. Money pits—It is very important to know how to spot potential problems that can be costly. Some of these are visible to the naked eye; some are not. Water damage, mold damage, some termite damage, and plumbing can be visible, and these properties should be avoided.

4. Inspections—It is always recommended that you obtain a home inspection from a professionally licensed home inspector before you purchase your real estate. This could save you thousands of dollars if an underlying structural problem, such as a cracked slab or faulty plumbing is found. The inspection will also assist you in making sure you obtain a complete list of needed repairs so your contractors can bid for the full of cost of those repairs. While they are not mandatory in most states, home inspections can be a good safety net for an investor. Whether you are spending $200,000 or $1,000,000, the minimal cost of a home inspection by a licensed, qualified home inspector is invaluable compared to the possible costs of hidden problems.

Some states do require specific inspections for radon, mold, water wells, or septic tanks. The most common inspections, however, are required from lenders and insurance companies. In any case, undisclosed problems become your problem after the purchase. Home inspectors are not regulated in over half the states within the United States. No licensing, schooling, continuing education, insurance, or previous experience is required in those states. Some states are heavily regulated, as they should be. Therefore, you need to be very diligent when searching for a home inspector and check your state laws to see what qualifications are mandatory in your area.

The two largest and most respected home inspection organizations are NACHI, the National Association of Certified Home Inspectors and ASHI, the American Society of Home Inspectors. These organizations require all applicants to be tested, to take continuing education courses annually, and to adhere to a strict code of ethics. Belonging to the Better Business Bureau and chamber of commerce will also show a company's commitment to quality within their community.

The contents of a home inspection report will highlight major visible defects and deficiencies. Home inspectors do not dismantle or disassemble any items covered in the report. The items noted are based on the apparent condition of visible and accessible areas at the time of the inspection.

Most home inspections will cover the foundation, siding, roof, mechanical systems (air-conditioning and furnace), windows, doors, electrical, plumbing, garage, all interior rooms, and the exterior of the home. In some states, but not all, appliances are checked to be sure they are functioning. Some inspectors will check the functioning of systems such as septic, water well, pool, sprinklers, hot tubs, etc. Other companies consider these items to be over and above the normal realm of a home inspection. If that is the case, professionals familiar with these areas should be asked to examine these systems.

The cost of a home inspection varies due to geographic location, square footage of the home, age of the home, and the amount of services required by the home inspector. An average price for inspecting a 2000 sq ft home will generally run from $300 to $500, depending on the age of the home and area of the country. There are no set prices, and they can vary tremendously. The first decision before submitting an offer to purchase an investment property should be to select your home inspector.

5. Expert advice—When you obtain bids from your contractors, ask them for cost-cutting suggestions, including materials such as lower grade floor coverings, outlet sources for appliances, etc. He/she may have a completely different opinion than you and can give you an idea of costs for repairs. Preparing a budget is paramount when repairing an investment property. It is important to focus on the fact that you are not creating a residence to suit your personal taste; rather, you are improving an investment property that will appeal to the largest market possible. It may not be a good financial decision to add some of the

more costly amenities, because they do not always add value or bring in more rental income.

6. Other people to listen to at this stage are good property managers or experienced investors who know the rental market. Property managers can give you an idea of which repairs or improvements will produce the best rental return. They can give you an idea of how to set the rental rate once it is finished. Don't set your mind on a preconceived number that the market may not bear; work within the parameters of the marketplace.

CHAPTER 8

Getting In and Getting Out

Edwin Kelly

For many of the richest American families, there have been three secrets for creating and keeping their wealth—compound interest, tax-deferred or tax-free dealings, and real estate investments.

Lest you think that these strategies are out of reach for the average person, let me put your mind at ease. Many investors are successfully earning 15–20%, even 25% and more, in their self-directed IRAs. I will show you how to keep compounding returns, tax-deferred or tax-free, for 100 years or more.

Few Americans realize that they have the option to self-direct their IRAs and other retirement plans into real estate—and that they can benefit from the tax advantages those plans provide. IRA investments earn tax-deferred or tax-free profits, depending on the type of IRA you select.

Combining the advantages of a self-directed IRA with your knowledge of real estate allows you to earn tax-free or tax-deferred returns on your investments.

The rate of return on your investments is based on your knowledge and expertise in real estate. Self-directed IRA investing in real estate is not based on the ups and downs of the stock market.

How can I buy real estate in my self-directed IRA?

In truth, there are all kinds of creative scenarios you could employ. But to make this simple, there are essentially three basic ways you can purchase real estate in your IRA.

1. The outright purchase

If you have sufficient funds in your self-directed IRA to cover the purchase price, closing costs, taxes, insurance, etc., you can purchase a property outright. All ongoing expenses must be paid exclusively from your self-directed IRA, and all income/profits must be returned only to the IRA. The foregoing assumes that the real estate is 100% owned by the IRA. Therefore, 100% of the profits must go to the IRA and 100% of the expenses must be paid by the IRA. In other words, no funds from outside the IRA (e.g., personal funds) can go into this investment.

When buying real estate outright in the IRA, it is important to remember to plan for the unexpected. If an expense pops up that you didn't anticipate, the money has to come from the IRA so the money should be available in some form or fashion. Remember, you cannot commingle your personal funds with your IRA funds.

2. The percentage or undivided interest

If you do not have sufficient funds in your self-directed IRA to cover the purchase price, closing costs, taxes, insurance reserves, etc., you have other options. The first one is having your IRA be a part owner in the investment. Let's assume your IRA has enough to be a 50% owner of the property. Then the IRA can hold a 50% ownership interest in the property and partner up with another IRA, person, or entity. In this scenario 50% of all ongoing expenses are paid from your self-directed IRA, and 50% of all income/profits are returned to your IRA. Because the real estate is 50% owned by the IRA, 50% of the profits must go to the IRA, and 50% of the expenses must be paid by the IRA. Any outside funds used have to remain in direct proportion to the percentage of ownership established at the outset. The same is true with IRA funds.

When buying an undivided interest in real estate, it is important to remember that the percentage of ownership determines how much money goes to and from the IRA. For example, let's say the real estate incurred a $1,000 plumbing expense. How much would need to be paid by the IRA? The answer is $500, 50% of the expense.

A common mistake that can easily be avoided is on the titling of the property. Remember, because this investment is owned not by you but by your IRA the titling would read: ABC Trust Company, Custodian FBO First Name Last Name, IRA, 50% Undivided Interest.

3. Leverage

If you do not have sufficient funds in your self-directed IRA to cover the purchase price, closing costs, taxes, insurance, etc., another very popular option is to use leverage, or debt inside of your self-directed IRA, to complete the investment. This is, in fact, how most people buy real estate personally, and it can be done within in the IRA as well. In this case, even though a minimum 30% equity is invested from the IRA, the property is still owned by and titled to the IRA like an outright purchase. The remaining 70% of the purchase price is financed using leverage (typically a non-recourse bank loan).

In this example, 100% of all expenses related to the investment would come from the IRA, and 100% of the revenue/profit would go to the IRA. It would still be prohibited to commingle personal funds with the IRA's funds, so having cash reserves in the account is always the best strategy.

Real estate scenarios

Those are the three basic ways to purchase real estate in your self-directed IRA. Another question that you are probably asking right about now is, "Well, that's how I can buy real estate in my IRA, but what kind of real estate can I invest in?"

The answer is, "What kind of real estate would you like to buy?" As long as you are making your investments in accordance with the IRS rules mentioned earlier, the only real limitation is your own creativity. Allow me to be a little more specific to get you pointed in the right direction.

For example, you can invest in

- Commercial property

- Single-family homes

- Condominiums

- Apartment buildings

- Foreclosures

- Pre-foreclosures

- Properties requiring repairs or rehab

As I said before, there are all kinds of creative spins for investing in real estate using your self-directed IRA. We will now look at a few of those. Remember, you cannot use these properties for personal use.

Short sale purchase process via your IRA

Pre-foreclosures are also known as a short sale purchase process, and this is one way you can acquire real estate in your IRA.

What is a short sale?

There is a period of time between when a borrower on a property becomes delinquent and the property is foreclosed. For judicial foreclosure proceedings, a lender will file suit against a borrower. The minimum time to a court ruling is 30 days; in some cases it can take many months before the foreclosure is completed. Investors can deal with the property owners to purchase the property during the foreclosure process, because the property is not yet owned by the bank. Let's look at one common example of how you could do this in your IRA.

Example: 123 Main Street, Anywhere, USA

- $110,000 Property Value

- $90,000 1st Lien with ABC Bank

- $20,000 2nd Lien with XYZ Bank

- $- 0 - Equity in property

The second lien holder knows that if this house sells at a low price, there is a risk of not being paid back and losing their entire loan balance. A second lien holder only receives sale proceeds if the first lien holder has been paid in full, and the sale proceeds are sufficient to cover the first mortgage and part or all of the second mortgage. As an investor, you can negotiate with the mortgage holder (bank) for a substantial loan discount on behalf of your IRA.

Typically, the second mortgage can be negotiated to a few thousand dollars so that equity is created (your IRA's profit), and, in many cases, you can negotiate a discount on the first mortgage as well. Let's assume, in this case, that we get the second lien holder to accept a $2,000 pay off and the first lien holder to take a 10% or $9,000 discount. We have just created $27,000 in potential equity and/or profit and will now have our IRA acquire the property for $83,000.

This scenario may seem outlandish, but when banks foreclose, especially in today's market, they know the property may sit vacant for many months, tying up their money and creating additional costs such as maintenance, real estate commissions, taxes, and attorney costs. If they can rid themselves of that expense, as well as the risk of having to keep the house on a long-term basis if it doesn't sell, that more than justifies giving a buyer a discount. The bank gets rid of the property, rid of the risk, and rid of the ongoing monthly expense. The investor gets instant equity. This is a win-win for all involved.

If you're a successful real estate investor, or if you're just looking to diversify your retirement portfolio, the combination of real estate and your IRA can be very powerful.

An IRA may obtain financing (loan/mortgage) for a real estate investment. However, keep in mind the following considerations:

- Do you have sufficient funds available in the IRA? If you are buying with 100% IRA funds (no leverage), and all funds are available in the IRA, then you may well be able purchase real estate.

- If you are using debt, the loan must be non-recourse. Per IRS regulations, an IRA cannot guarantee a loan nor can the IRA balance be used as collateral. A non-recourse loan only uses the real estate and leases for collateral to secure repayment of the loan. In the event of default, the lender can only collect the property through foreclosure and cannot collect from the IRA account balance or the owner of the IRA.

- Tax is due on profits from leveraged real estate. If your IRA uses debt financing (i.e., obtains a loan) on a real estate investment, a tax will probably be due on profits. This tax is called unrelated business income tax (UBIT) as explained in chapter 5.

What is the process of making an investment like this?

The process for making an investment like this is actually simple and straightforward. It involves only three steps, and you will be on your way to a diversified retirement portfolio.

1. Open a self-directed retirement account.

This can be done literally in a matter of minutes. An application for a self-directed IRA is typically one to two pages long and asks for your basic information that you have readily available. The key is to make sure you select a self-directed IRA custodian. Most custodians do not offer the option to direct your own retirement account, so you must move your funds to one that does. Remember that some larger institutions have been calling their IRA accounts "self-directed" when they are not. They are referring to the fact that you can choose which of their investments you want to hold in the account, but this does not mean they will allow you to hold real estate. Be sure your self-directed IRA custodian will allow real estate transactions.

2. Put money in the account.

The second step in the process is to "fund" or put money in the account. There are four ways:

- First, you can make a contribution. To make a contribution, all you need is earned income. You simply write a check and deposit it into your self-directed IRA.

- Second, you can do an IRA rollover. If you have an old 401(k), 403(b), or other plan from a previous employer, you can roll that money into your self-directed IRA.

- Third, you can do a transfer (full or partial) from another IRA. If you have an IRA at a traditional financial institution like a bank or a brokerage house, you can transfer all (full) or some (partial) of the money to your self-directed IRA.

- Finally, you can, in some cases, do an IRA conversion. This is where money from one type of an IRA, such as a traditional IRA is converted into a different IRA such as a Roth IRA.

3. Make an investment.

Here is the magic in the process. This is where you communicate to your self-directed IRA custodian the investments you want to purchase with your account after considering your investment options. I say it's magic because this is the step that makes your account truly self-directed and under your control.

And there you have it. You have just completed your first self-directed IRA investment. Well, almost. We have acquired an investment like the short sale we just walked through, but we haven't realized any profit yet. Seasoned investors will tell you the day to celebrate is the day you buy, not the day you sell, because you really make your money the day you invest in real estate if you have done your investment research and purchased the property at the right price.

Exit strategies

Let's assume you have acquired the real estate in your IRA. Now, what do you do with it? You may choose to rent it out for many years, or you may choose to fix it up and sell it immediately. Either way, you need to have an exit strategy or a way of getting cash out of the property. I will show you three ways to pull cash out of the property and have it flow back to your IRA.

1. Retailing

Retailing is a strategy where you will sell the property at or close to fair-market value to an end buyer or the new homeowner. For a property to be retailed properly, it will need to be in good condition. Typically, such investment sales will have been rehabbed and staged to sell at full market value for maximum profits. Retail properties are usually bought at a discount, rehabbed, and then staged and put on the market, sometimes with a real estate agent. The goal is to maximize profits by finding a buyer to pay maximum market value. In the case above, where you acquired the real estate in the IRA as a foreclosure from a bank and created $27,000 in equity, the goal would be to sell the property at or close to fair market value and realize the full $27,000 in profit. The advantage to retailing is that it can yield the largest dollar return. The potential downside is that it may take longer to realize the profit, and because the IRA is responsible for all rehab costs, anything unexpected will be the responsibility of the IRA.

2. Wholesaling

There are two definitions of "wholesaling" when it comes to real estate. The first (and original) definition means buying a property and quickly reselling it for a profit. Usually, the property is distressed in some way, and you'll be reselling it to a rehabber who will renovate the property, and will then resell the property to a new owner.

The second definition of "wholesaling" is purchasing the distressed property and rehabbing it quickly as possible. This usually means hiring a contractor and having a crew repair the house under the investor's supervision. Then, once the property is rehabbed, it is sold. This newest definition has only recently come in to existence due to popular television programs, such as "Flip This House," on the Home and Garden channel.

Let's go back to our example where our IRA owns a property and we have created $27,000 in equity. Using a wholesaling strategy, we may sell the property at a markup where our IRA receives a $5,000 profit, and the remaining $22,000 is realized by the next investor. The advantage of wholesaling is that we can realize a quicker profit with little or no responsibility for the repairs to the property. We also need less money because we don't incur any costs or risks associated with the rehab. The trade-off is that we get fewer dollars in the IRA as a result of reducing the investment risk.

3. Lease options

An alternative financing option is one that allows the tenant to lease a home from your self-directed IRA with an option to purchase at a later date. Each month's rent payment may consist of the market rent, plus an additional amount which can be applied toward the down payment on a specified price settled at the time of lease.

The advantage is that we will sell the property retail and realize a greater profit than our wholesale method. In other words, the option to purchase the property may be two years in the future, so you can agree upon the purchase price, assuming appreciation over the next two years. Additionally, there would be positive cash flow back to the IRA from the rent payments.

Using our short-sale example, let's assume the value of 123 Main Street is going to appreciate 5% the next 2 years. The agreed-upon sale price would be $121,275. In this example we have now increased the cash return back to our IRA: $121,275 –$83,000 = $38,275. This doesn't include the positive monthly cash flow or the nonrefundable purchase option consideration we received in the beginning of the lease giving the tenant the right to purchase the property. These two things combined could add an additional $4,400, increasing our total cash back to the IRA of $42,675, plus we made the sale without paying a real estate commission. Best of all, because we are doing this in our IRA, all of our realized profits will grow tax-deferred or tax-free, depending on the type of IRA we are using!

Compounding real estate investments in the self-directed Roth IRA

One of the greatest gifts our government has given us is the Roth IRA. Let's look at what would happen when we combine the power of real estate with a self-directed Roth IRA.

I will assume you are 38 years old. Let's take our investment of $83,000 from our Main Street investment. Let's also assume we were able to compound our money at 14% over time. How much would your Roth IRA be worth at age 65? The answer—hold on to your socks—is $3,558,024. That's if you never made another contribution to the account!

What if you did not use the Roth IRA and went with a taxable real estate investment? Then, much of your profit would be donated to the IRS. How much, you ask? Well, if we assume a 25% tax bracket after you pay taxes, you would be left with less than $1.5 million. Which amount of money would you rather have? That is the power of tax-free compounding during your accumulation phase.

The hidden magic of compounding during distribution

While much has been said about the wonders of compound interest during the accumulation years of an IRA plan, surprisingly little has been said about the effects of tax-deferred or tax-free compounding during the distribution stage of an IRA. The effect of this later interest buildup can be considerably more significant than the effect of the earlier compounding because of the much greater sums of money involved. If the annual tax-deferred contributions can make you a millionaire in 25 years while you are working, your accumulated funds can make you a multimillionaire over the next 25 years, after you retire, without contributing another dime. In fact, your funds can do this and still pay you handsome annual distributions along the way.

If you do not live long enough to use your self-directed IRA funds, several possibilities exist for what happens to the money in your account. When you start a self-directed IRA, you designate a beneficiary. When you die, your beneficiary, if a spouse, may choose any of the following options: (1) withdraw IRA funds as a lump sum, which may be taxable during that year; (2) take yearly distributions based on his or her life expectancy; (3) use a portion of the money for current needs, after paying taxes, and roll over the balance; or (4) convert the IRA into his or her own account. The new owner will have all the rights and obligations of the former owner.

Most spouses choose to roll over the money left to them into their own IRA. However, if the beneficiary is not a spouse, he or she has only five years to take all funds out of the account, or the money is distributed over the life expectancy of the beneficiary.

How long can an IRA last?

An IRA could last 100 years or more. Take the example of a 35-year-old man. His IRA account compounds tax-deferred until he reaches age 70½. That's 35 years. Shortly thereafter, he dies; his spouse, who is 70, inherits the IRA and lives until age 80½. That's another 10 years.

Finally, the couple's son or daughter or other individual beneficiary inherits the IRA at the age of 35. Assuming he or she lives a full life expectancy (age 85), that adds another 55 years to the previous total of 45 years. That's a grand total of 100 years. Even though some distribution occurs, tax-deferred compounding applies to the income and profits earned during all of those 100 years.

Using strategies like these is how America's richest families pass wealth to their heirs. You can use these same strategies to pass wealth to your children and grandchildren.

CHAPTER 9

Prohibited Transactions

Tom Anderson

Before we begin exploring the do's and don'ts of self-directed IRA investing, including those associated with the use of leverage, it is important to understand what a self-directed IRA is and isn't. The term "self-directed" is not a technical or legal term, but rather a descriptive term about how the IRA is managed. "Self-directed" essentially means that the IRA owner, or someone the IRA owner appoints, makes all the investment choices and decisions for the IRA. One can have a self-directed IRA at a brokerage firm or with a specialist firm which is a self-directed IRA custodian. The primary difference is that brokerage firms and traditional banks that offer self-directed IRA services generally restrict investments to publicly-traded assets such as stocks and mutual funds.

The second important thing to know about self-directed IRAs is that they may belong only to a single individual person and are unique by taxpayer ID. Except for some IRAs established for employees in an employment context, the IRAs are not subject to ERISA, so the restrictions placed on fiduciaries of pension plans subject to ERISA (such as prudence, diversification standards, and foreign investment restrictions), generally do not apply to IRAs. IRAs are governed by IRC section 408, whereas pension plans are governed by IRC sections 401, 403, and 457.

Because IRA investments are not restricted by law to traditional assets like stocks and mutual funds, there are innumerable ways to invest through self-directed IRAs and an unlimited array of investment choices. That's the good news. However, there are some investment types and transactions that are prohibited that you must be aware of in order to avoid jeopardizing the status of your IRA and exposing it and you to taxes and penalties. This chapter will review the basic tax rules on IRA investing, while providing you with a general understanding of the legal framework from which the rules flow.

The basics

First of all, the basics of what not to do can be generally and easily summarized by saying that there are three asset types that you can't invest in, and that neither you nor any other "disqualified person" may, under the tax laws, engage in self-dealing with your IRA. Other than the explanation of the details behind the last sentence, that's what you need to know in a nutshell. Self-dealing means essentially that you or other "disqualified persons" may not use your IRA to obtain a personal benefit other than what you receive as a by-product of your IRA's growth. This is not rocket science as some detractors would claim. For example, I am not a rocket scientist, just a banker, and I understand the rules. So relax; you can, too.

I find, however, that the biggest challenge is accepting the reality of the rules, because they prevent many from doing what they would like to do to obtain the maximum amount of benefit from their IRA investing. The problem is, particularly for those investing in real estate, that many have the desire to make personal use of the properties that their IRAs purchase (e.g., a vacation home). However, you may not, because that would be a blatant example of self-dealing and a violation of the rules. There are no workarounds for "trying to have your cake and eat it too."

Fundamentally, you should understand that IRAs were created as part of The Employee Retirement Income Security Act (ERISA) in 1974 (the primary purpose of which was to bolster and reform the pension laws) to provide individuals an alternative way to save for retirement. Benefits, in the form of increasing contribution limits and more flexibility in transporting retirement funds between the various types of pension plans, have increased over time as the government began recognizing the importance of IRAs as part of an individual's overall retirement plan. That recognition, of not only the importance of IRAs to their owners, but the overall size of the IRA market ($3.6 trillion in 2009), has stimulated increased interest on the part of the IRS and the Department of Labor (DOL), and the latter has jurisdiction over determining prohibited transactions.

Who can hold your self-directed IRA?

The IRS's interest in IRAs is fundamental. It has jurisdiction over the Internal Revenue Code that defines and governs IRAs, including determining which institutions are eligible to maintain custody of them. Essentially, any bank, credit union, or state-chartered financial institution (e.g., trust company) is automatically qualified to have custody of IRAs based on their approval and acceptance by a regulating body such as a state banking commissioner or the FDIC, etc. Any institution not in that class must apply to and be approved by the IRS in order to be a custodian of IRAs. There are currently about 250 such institutions, called "nonbank custodians," so approved in the United States today (e.g., broker/dealers, mutual funds companies). If you aren't in a "banking" group, or approved by the IRS, then you may not offer IRA custodial services directly. If you place your IRA with an institution that is not authorized as described above, you face the risk that your IRA will be invalidated and that you will be subject to taxes and penalties. So, a word to the wise: please be sure to determine that the institution with which you place your IRA is duly chartered in one of the two alternative classes described above.

What can't you invest in?

While it is essential that the institution that holds your IRA is authorized to do so, the likelihood that you find yourself with a firm that is not so authorized is slim. But, in any event, there are several types of actions that you, as the IRA owner, could inadvertently or deliberately take that are impermissible. The simplest one to describe has to do with the type of investment you make with your IRA.

As previously alluded to, there are only three types of investments that your IRA *cannot* make: (1) collectibles (e.g., stamps, antique furniture, jewelry, most coins, art, rugs, 1957 Corvettes, etc.), or anything the U.S. Treasury deems to be a collectible; (2) life insurance; and (3) the stock of a subchapter S corporation.

In terms of collectibles there are many other examples (not specifically defined in the IRS code) of what the IRS and DOL might consider a collectible. For example, gold coins (other than coins minted by the U.S. mint, e.g., American Gold eagles) such as Kruggerands are not permitted investments. In addition, the view by the Treasury Department of a given investment can vary from day to day and department to department depending on whom you speak with and the day of the week. I once had a broker from Merrill Lynch call me and ask if his client could purchase a brand-new, limited-edition Ford GT muscle car ($150,000) with his IRA. Initially, because this was not an antique, and because the client's stated intent was to resell it for a profit after holding it for a while as an investment, I thought it was worthwhile to call the DOL and ask their opinion.

The DOL representative, a well-known and respected member of the organization, replied that "On a good day, they probably wouldn't consider the asset a collectible. However, on a bad day, they might consider it a prohibited transaction because they would be afraid the IRA owner would make personal use of the GT and drive it to the next Concourse 'D Elegance." The DOL representative then suggested I call his associate in the IRS hierarchy to get his opinion. After making that call, the IRS representative essentially said the same thing: "On a good day ..." So naturally, I called the Merrill Lynch broker back to sum up and report the essence of my research, by saying "On a good day!"

We know that an IRA owner cannot purchase a life insurance policy on his own life, nor anything deemed a collectible:

- **Artwork,**

- **Rugs,**

- Antiques,

- Metals,

- Gems,

- Stamps,

- Alcoholic beverages, and

- Certain other tangible property (the infamous catch-22, such as a 1957 Corvette).

- Coins: An exception allows your IRA to invest in one, one-half, one-quarter, or one-tenth ounce U.S. gold coins, and one-ounce silver coins minted by the Treasury Department. It can also invest in certain platinum coins and certain gold, silver, palladium, and platinum bullion.

Is there anything else that an IRA cannot invest in? No! However, before you get too excited, there is another problematic investment or asset type for those who have an IRA, the stock of a subchapter S corporation. While it is not a prohibited transaction for the IRA to make a purchase of the stock of a sub S corporation, it is prohibited for the S corporation. Simply stated, an S corporation is not permitted to have an IRA as a shareholder. In fact, the consequence of an S corporation allowing and having an IRA investor is the loss of the status as an S corporation. That is, there is a very limited time that an S corporation can "undo" such an investment by an IRA before it becomes a C corporation, which is an event that would no doubt make other S shareholders quite unhappy, for reasons beyond the scope of this book. Suffice it to say, if you are contemplating investing your IRA in your nephew's new S corporation with your IRA, forget it. If you want to extend a loan to an S corporation with your IRA, in most cases, you'll be able to do that. Later in this chapter I will explain when doing so would also be considered a prohibited transaction that will have to do with IRC code section 4975 (the entire code is included in the Additional Resources section).

What are "prohibited transactions"?

Quite frankly, everyone now understands that with the exception of three asset types discussed above, you can invest in anything with an IRA, and the fact is, you have been able to do so since 1974, when IRAs were first created! Just to expand your mind on the possibilities, I'll list a few unusual items that self-directed IRA investors have invested in over the years:

- boat slips

- 40 head of cattle

- fishing rights for sablefish in the State of Alaska

- a massage school

- bankruptcy claims

- a fraternity

- a Cypress tree farm in Costa Rica

- a condo in Croatia

- two acres of land in New Zealand

- a pizza parlor

- a de novo (startup) bank

- a major web-based business

- a gas station

- a nudist colony

- a restaurant

- a small plot of land 3 miles off shore of Miami Beach and 60 feet under water -housing a graveyard designed to look like the fabled city of Atlantis, and approved by the EPA (long story)

- and thousands of others, including the tens of thousands more traditional real estate and private equity investments!

Most people who first hear about the possibilities react with shock. For years, they have heard from traditional IRA providers that such investments with IRAs were illegal, extremely complicated and expensive, very risky, or any combination of the above. Some are outright angry when they learn the truth; knowing that they were ill-informed and, in many cases, as a result, deprived of an investment opportunity they felt was very promising. I have actually spoken to new clients who have indicated that they were going to pursue legal action against their broker or CPA who told them a given desired transaction was illegal! Rest assured that all of the above investments and possible investment types, are legal provided that the nature of the transaction between their IRA and the investment itself does not violate the prohibited transaction rules that we are now going to explore.

First, let me say that there is one fundamental rule that applies to all IRA investments. That rule, the exclusive benefit rule, states that only the IRA can benefit from the transaction. That makes sense when you think about the fundamental purpose of an IRA. The government created IRAs at the same time it passed legislation (ERISA) to put controls over employer-sponsored pension plans to prevent abuses by fiduciaries who were misusing or stealing the pension funds of their employees.

To give additional control and options to future retirees, the government created IRAs to allow them to save for retirement independently from employer-sponsored plans. Unfortunately, the government had to step in again 30 years later with the Pension Protection Act of 2006 to prevent new abuses such as what happened to wipe out Enron and WorldCom employees' retirement accounts.

But what do we mean by the exclusive benefit rule in the real world? Basically, neither the IRA owner nor any other "disqualified person" may receive a personal benefit as a result of a transaction by his or her IRA.

It is almost that simple if not for the plan asset rule, and other elements of IRC 4975, which I will discuss later as well as certain IRS notices, Department of Labor rulings, and court cases. For example, you cannot extend a loan from your IRA to yourself or any direct relative (remember "disqualified person"), even though (believe it or not), because of a

Department of Labor (DOL) Prohibited Transaction Exemption (PTE) called 80-26, you can actually lend money to your own IRA in limited circumstances!

Prohibited transactions and real estate investing

I would like to explain some of the typical scenarios involving real estate and self-directed IRA investing that can result in prohibited transactions. It seems that whenever someone finds out that they can buy real estate in their retirement account, they assume that they can use the property. This is natural because real estate investing has been done primarily through the use of disposable income, where there is no restriction on use. However, there is a fundamental difference when an IRA is involved. The rules in place make it very clear that an IRA owner cannot make personal use of any of his IRA's assets (*any* IRA asset, including real estate) without incurring a prohibited transaction. For example, one basic example of a violation of the exclusive benefit rule would be purchasing a vacation home for personal use. No, you can't vacation in your IRA-owned vacation home (even for a weekend). Furthermore, you can't use the property, even if you pay rent, because from the government's perspective you are receiving a personal benefit. You can't even buy raw land and hunt on it with your buddies.

There are many more examples of less direct cases of receiving a personal benefit as a by-product of your IRA's investment that deserve mention. I have found when it comes to self-directed IRAs, that, in addition to incorrect information in the public and professional arenas, there is a lack of information.

At this point, I would say, that 95+% of IRA transactions conducted by regulated self-directed IRA custodians are straightforward. One of the things I ask attendees at presentations I give on prohibited transactions is "How many people own their personal residence?" As you can imagine, the vast majority of hands rise in response. I then ask "How many of those who have raised their hands purchased the home you live in from a direct family member?" Without exception, more than 99% of the time, all the hands go down. The analogy is that if you are purchasing a rental property from a third-party that you will then rent to someone who is also a third party (not a "disqualified person"), and there is no other self-dealing go on, that you'll have no issues with prohibited transactions.

If you are paying attention, you'll want to know what I mean by "no other self-dealing going on." Let me use an example that will clarify what I mean. Suppose you agree to have your IRA purchase a rental property from someone you are not directly related to, and then you rent it to another person you are also not related to. This seems okay, right? There are no disqualified persons and no personal benefit. Your IRA will receive the rent, and you will not. Yes, this is fine. However, suppose this agreement is matched by the person you are renting to, and the person agrees with you to have his/her IRA or personal funds buy another rental property that the person will then rent to you. This type of preconceived quid pro quo is called a "stepped" or "linked" transaction by the IRS, because in their minds, it is nothing more than a scheme to avoid an otherwise prohibited transaction, and is, therefore, tantamount to a prohibited transaction and thus will be treated as such in this case.

The consequence will be that you and your friend's IRAs will be treated as distributed to you and your friend at the fair market value retroactively determined as of the first day of the year of the prohibited transaction. If the only assets in your respective IRAs are the rental properties, the tax laws then will treat you as owning the properties personally, not in your IRAs.

Let's review another typical real estate scenario where you want to use your IRA as a down payment in conjunction with a loan to purchase a property. Doing so involves the use of a non-recourse loan, as previously discussed. The IRA rules require that the loan be non-recourse because a typical homeowner loan has recourse for you as a borrower. However, because you are a disqualified person in relation to your IRA, you cannot enable or "help out" your IRA by providing your guarantee or your IRA's loan. That would be self-dealing with your IRA. Similarly, although you are permitted to co-invest with your IRA and yourself and other disqualified persons on an all-cash real estate purchase, you cannot co-invest and assume a debt along with your IRA because your personal capital is helping to secure the loan, and, once again, that would be self-dealing. On the other hand, if your IRA wants to buy a property with leverage by joining with an unrelated third party (e.g., a personal friend), you may do so because the friend is not a disqualified person. For example, your IRA puts in 20% of the purchase price, the friend 15%, and the bank loan finances the remaining 65%. This is permitted. However, substituting your personal money for your friend's 15% is not.

Another typical and potentially problematic area involves the management of property owned by your IRA. Neither you nor any other disqualified person is permitted to provide goods and services for your IRA. Typically, real property requires maintenance (repairs) or management (finding and dealing with tenants and rents, etc.). Under the rules, you are not permitted to provide more than ministerial services to manage your IRA-owned assets. The rules are not specific about all those activities that might be considered ministerial versus "goods and services"; however, in general, you can act as a traffic cop in directing the activities of other unrelated parties who can then provide goods and services to your IRA-owned asset (e.g., repair a roof). General practice is that you would select a vendor and submit a bill upon completion or in advance to your IRA custodian, with instructions to pay the bill from your IRA. You cannot pay the direct expenses related to the maintenance of the property, even if your IRA later reimburses you. The IRA has to be responsible for such expenses. Once again, however, in addition to making additional contributions to your IRA or adding and consolidating funds from other personal IRAs to provide necessary funds, you may also *lend* money to your IRA for emergency expenses.

You are able to direct all the activities surrounding your IRA investment and, for example, select vendors and tenants. Just don't go over and fix the toilet in your rental property, assuming you're so inclined. Also, don't use your real estate company's tractor to plow a right of way on your IRA-owned property or take a commission on the sale of your IRA-owned property because you are a real estate broker. You can hire your nephew (not a disqualified person) to clean the gutters. It is advisable when you employ anyone who might be considered a party-in-interest or someone you might be emotionally attached to (e.g., fiancé) that you do so at a fair market price to avoid any appearance of self-dealing.

Finally, if you have a property that you might be considering for conversion to an IRA from a pension plan or a traditional IRA, don't try to save some tax dollars by asking someone to give you a low (below market) valuation. If you are later audited by the IRS, they will frown upon not getting their pound of flesh in terms of tax revenues and might charge you with tax evasion. Get an independent appraisal from a legitimate appraisal firm, not your brother-in-law.

I guess you are getting a little frustrated now that you know there are no gimmicks to get around a prohibited transaction that the IRS hasn't seen and hasn't prevented by statute. You'll get over it when you realize the substantial benefits of self-directed IRAs covered elsewhere in this book. But first, you need to be aware of pitfalls to avoid so you can preserve the integrity of your retirement savings.

The consequences of engaging in a prohibited transaction

I know of a doctor who was being audited by the IRS who was taxed and penalized for parking his car on his IRA-owned lot that was adjacent to the building that he worked in. The consequences of engaging in a prohibited transaction are serious. In simple terms, the consequence for an IRA owner or beneficiary engaging in a prohibited transaction is severe. No, you don't go directly to jail to get measured for an orange jumpsuit. In fact, you don't go to jail at all unless you fail to pay the tax due to the IRS and, are, therefore, guilty of tax evasion. But you lose the tax-exempt status of your IRA from the first day of the year in which the prohibited transaction occurs, resulting in a taxable distribution of your entire IRA balance (unless it is a Roth, in which case only the earnings the IRA earned up to the time of the deemed distribution are taxed), plus a 10% penalty if this occurs before you are age 59½, plus penalties and interest if the taxes weren't paid on time!

How do you determine if you are creating a prohibited transaction?

One of the first things you can do is identify all of the players involved in the IRA. First, there is your IRA (which will fund the investment); then, there is you (the IRA owner), and, by definition, a disqualified person. Are there any other disqualified persons involved in any way with the outcome of this investment? Are you getting any benefit personally from your IRA's transaction? An example may be helpful to explain how this could occur, even innocently.

Suppose you are a real estate broker, many of whom, because of their real estate knowledge and interest, use their IRAs to purchase real estate. You find a seller with a nice property that you'd like to buy with your IRA. Of course, as a real estate broker working on the seller's behalf, you are due a commission. Is it going to create a prohibited transaction if you collect a commission on this transaction? What do you think? Yes, taking a commission on a purchase involving your IRA will constitute a prohibited transaction because you are personally receiving a benefit from your IRA's transaction.

Suppose you are selling a property that your IRA owns. Can you then charge your IRA a commission? No, you cannot for the same reasons as in the first example. Staying with this basic example, suppose your son was also a broker with your firm. Could he sell the property to your IRA and take a commission? No, he can't because he is a disqualified person in relation to you and your IRA because he is your descendant.

Suppose you don't take a commission, but you handle the sale. Is that OK? Maybe. As long as you are just performing ministerial duties (e.g., basic paperwork) and are not providing the types of professional services that normally would be compensated for, you should be fine. However, it is probably advisable to have some other broker in your office (unrelated to you) handle the sale. That broker can then get a commission, provided you don't personally benefit from their receipt of the commission (e.g., as you might if you were the owner of the real estate firm for which you and he/she work).

Can you have an understanding with that broker that he will do the same thing with his IRA, allowing you to obtain a commission by selling property to his IRA? You should know the answer to that by now. Yes, you are correct in assuming that doing so would be considered a "stepped" transaction. Any such similar quid pro quo arrangements that are designed to avoid directly running afoul of prohibited transactions will not pass an IRS or DOL examination.

Many people suggest that it should be okay if their IRA deals with a disqualified person as long as there is no advantage gained over what might be obtained by two unrelated parties engaging in the same transaction. That is, the transaction is consummated at true fair market value. They would add that their IRA benefits financially in the deal. Unfortunately, unless you request and obtain a prohibited transaction exemption (PTE) from the Department of Labor *before you engage in the transaction,* you will no doubt fail to prevail in an IRS audit with that argument.

One of the reasons for that, and one of the sections of the IRC that has a significant impact on the ability to transact freely with your IRA, is IRC section 4975. Spending a little time reviewing this IRC section should help give you perspective on how the IRS or DOL might react to an investment scenario if you were ever audited (an infrequent event, but one possible to avoid), because of the cost of a negative outcome, which I have previously discussed.

As I mentioned, the fact that a transaction between a disqualified person (e.g., buying a condo with your IRA for your daughter to use while attending college) was executed at fair market value is insufficient to protect the transaction from being considered prohibited is primarily because of the rules within IRC 4975. Therefore, it is essential that we cover the main points of this IRC section. First, generally speaking, any transaction between an IRA and a disqualified person (owner, spouse of owner, lineal ascendants and descendants, and spouses of lineal descendants, for the most part) is a prohibited transaction. Siblings, ironically, are not disqualified persons. Specifically, the IRC prohibits any:

- **sale or exchange between an IRA and a disqualified person;**

- **loan or other extension of credit between an IRA and a disqualified person;**

- furnishing of goods, services, or facilities between an IRA and a disqualified person;

- act by a disqualified person who is a fiduciary whereby he deals with the income or assets of a plan in his own interest or for his own account; or

- receipt of any consideration for his own personal account by any disqualified person who is a fiduciary from any party dealing with the plan in connection with a transaction involving the income or assets of the plan.

In layman's terms, and by example, you cannot use your IRA to buy ("sale or exchange") your father's farm when he retires, extend a loan ("extension of credit") to your son for the down payment on the purchase of his first home, or park your car on the vacant lot ("facilities") owned by your IRA.

Here is a quick overview of the elements that may create a prohibited transaction:

1. A plan (pension) or an IRA;

2. A "disqualified person"; and

3. A transaction between 1 and 2 above.

However, IRC 4975 goes on to say that, in addition to the previously defined list of "disqualified persons" in relation to IRAs, the following are also classified as disqualified persons:

- Any entity that is 50% or more controlled or 50% or more beneficially owned (including attribution of ownership from family members, certain partners, and through other entities) by the IRA's owner;

- Any officer, director, 10% shareholder, partner, or individual earning 10% or more of the annual wages of an entity identified in 1; or

- Any IRA trustee or custodian and/or service provider and individuals and entities related to them.

The IRS is saying that if your interest, including any indirect interest through specified relatives, etc., is equal to 50% or more in an entity, your IRA may not transact with that entity, because the entity *itself* is thereby deemed to be a disqualified person. If you and your wife owned 49% of an entity and the remaining 51% was owned by unrelated partners or entities, then you or your wife's IRA could potentially buy out the other partners to end up owning 100% of the entity if you wanted!

The key is that, at the time of transaction execution, you can't have a preexisting interest of 50% or more. In terms of the second point, if the entity is deemed to be a disqualified person by virtue of satisfying item one above, then your IRA cannot transact with these individuals whose circumstance match or exceed those outlined in point two. Finally, you cannot deal with your IRA (nor can the entities listed in point three above). For example, you cannot co-invest with the custodian of your IRA. The Pension Protection Act of 2006, however, enacted a new exemption that allowed certain sales and loans with nonfiduciary service providers if certain conditions are met.

With all that bad news, is there anything you can do? Of course. Remember, in the normal course of investing you are not dealing with people who are your relatives. For example, when you bought the house you live in, did you buy it from a direct relative? Probably not anymore than would be the case if your IRA purchased a rental property. Furthermore, there are certain classes and statutory exemptions that can be obtained for otherwise prohibited transactions. In other words, you may be eligible for an individual exemption before you proceed with a transaction you suspect to be prohibited. Many of these individual exemption requests are granted. However, bear in mind that they do not serve as legal precedents in relation to any subsequent transactions by either the person granted the exemption or anyone else for that matter.

One interesting exemption that many are not aware of is that an individual IRA owner or other disqualified person can extend an interest-free, unsecured loan to an IRA for either a purpose incidental to the ordinary operation of the IRA, or for payment of ordinary operating expenses, including payment of benefits! This exemption can be found in PTE class

Exemption 80-26 (and related 2002-13). So if you held a rental property in your IRA that you had a mortgage on and you lost your tenant, you probably could lend money to your IRA to pay the mortgage. Ironically, you cannot pay the mortgage personally for your IRA, though. Also, under this exemption, you cannot lend money to augment or support a new investment not held in your account at the time of the loan. Also, besides the requirement that the loan be noninterest-bearing, be aware that if the loan to the IRA will be outstanding more than 60 days, the IRA owner must provide the IRA custodian with a note, indicating the debt obligation by the IRA to its owner.

A statutory exception under IRC 4975(d) (2) allows for a contract or reasonable arrangement between an IRA and a disqualified person for office space, or legal, accounting, or other services necessary for the establishment or operation of the IRA, provided no more than reasonable compensation is paid. However, other rules generally prohibit the disqualified person from receiving compensation for permitted services. On the other hand, "sweat equity" might be viewed as "imputed income," which can also be a problem. Generally, because of overlapping and contradictory rules, it is not advisable, without legal advice, to have any transaction with a disqualified person.

Co-investment rules

One of the important things to understand is that, in most cases, your IRA may co-invest with disqualified persons including yourself, friends, family, third parties (including entities), and any other IRAs or pension plans you may have. DOL Advisory Opinion 2000-10A outlines the caveats, however, including the fact that you have to be in a position to prove that you could have accomplished the transaction without the use of your IRA (to avoid a prohibited transaction for enabling) if you are ever challenged. For example, if you have additional financial resources that could be used (e.g., a home equity loan, another qualified pension plan or IRA, a stock brokerage account, etc.), but you chose your IRA to co-invest with because it was convenient or because it was a good investment for the IRA, you should be okay. The advisory also warned that a prohibited transaction could occur if a conflict between the IRA and IRA owner develops at some point and the IRA owner fails to resolve it. Unfortunately, no examples or acceptable solutions are provided.

It is important that co-investment involving disqualified persons is executed simultaneously. For example, you can't purchase a home for your son with your IRA one week and have him compensate you or your IRA the next (either directly or by investing in the property). But if your IRA and your son jointly purchased the home, provided there is no debt, and you purchase the property from someone other than a disqualified person, that's fine.

Department of Labor (DOL) plan asset rules

The DOL's plan asset rules essentially define when the assets of an entity are considered "plan" assets (under the laws, IRAs are frequently treated as pension plans, as in this case). If aggregate plan and IRA ownership of any class of equity interests in an entity is 25% or more, the assets of the entity are viewed as assets of the investing IRA or plan for purposes of the prohibited transactions rules, unless an exception applies. Among the exceptions are public investment companies and "operating companies," such as companies that either invest in real estate development, venture capital, or companies making or providing goods and services (e.g., a gas station, grocery store, restaurant, etc.).

One example can help to explain how the plan asset rules come into play when analyzing the potential for a prohibited transaction between an entity with plan investors and a disqualified person in relation to one or more of those plans. Let's assume you have a general partner of a hedge fund who also wishes to invest his IRA in the hedge fund he manages.

If the percentage of IRA and plan ownership, including what it would be after the general partner invests his IRA in the fund, equals or exceeds 25% of any class of equity interests, then the fund's assets are considered "plan assets." That means that a transaction between him, as a disqualified person, and the fund could be deemed a prohibited transaction because the assets of the entity are viewed as assets of his IRA, and as we know, a disqualified person cannot transact with the assets of his plan or IRA.

Because of this, the general partner, cannot receive benefits from his IRA (a fund investor). Thus the general partner would need to exempt his IRA from fees he would otherwise charge, because he would be receiving a personal benefit from his IRA.

There are a couple of interesting quirks to the plan asset rules. For one, the IRA attribution rules apparently do not apply to the plan asset rules; thus, it is arguable that the assets of an entity owned 95% by an IRA and 5% by the IRA owner, provided it was an operating company, would not be considered plan assets. The DOL plan asset rules only talk of related plans, and not parties that are not plans that may also be related to the plans.

Second, the DOL has taken the position that, even if the assets of an entity are not plan assets of an IRA, a prohibited transaction could still occur if a disqualified person of that IRA enters into a prearranged deal to obtain a personal benefit (e.g., an employment contract) from the company as a result of his IRA's investment in the company. (That was the finding in the Department of Labor's 2006-1A finding that will be discussed later.) This brings the importance of the plan asset rule into question.

IRS wants to control Roth IRA abuses

There are active investigations by the IRS into abuses of Roth IRAs. Because Roth IRA distributions are potentially exempt from income tax, the IRS is concerned that taxpayers will self-deal or over-contribute to maximize their gains from the tax-free aspects of Roth IRAs and to avoid the limitations on Roth IRA contributions. To the IRS, this is not clever strategizing by the taxpayer, but tax evasion! A case in point is provided by a scenario in IRS Notice 2004-8.

In this scenario, a Roth IRA owner, a business he owned, and a corporation substantially owned by his Roth IRA, were involved in a transaction. The Roth-owned company received property from the company owned by the Roth IRA owner. The IRS issued guidance (Notice 2004-8; IRB 2004-4) which is designed to shut down abuses involving indirect contributions to Roth IRAs.

Apparently, a well-known accounting firm, which shall remain nameless, decided to write in the *Wall Street Journal* about what they thought was a well-designed tax shelter strategy, only to learn that the IRS disagreed. The result was an IRS Notice indicating that such strategies were considered abuses and, therefore, dictated the U.S. Treasury Department list-keeping and registration requirements for tax shelter arrangements that are "listed transactions."

The guidance addresses situations in which value is shifted into an individual's Roth IRA through transactions involving entities owned by the individual and certain related persons. For example, a business owned by the individual could sell its receivables for less than fair value to a shell corporation owned by the individual's Roth IRA.

This scheme artificially shifts taxable income away from the individual's business into the shelter of the Roth IRA structure. The IRS said, "In effect, this is a disguised contribution to the Roth IRA and the notice makes clear that it will be treated as such." Furthermore, in the scenario discussed in IRS Notice 2004-8, the value shift was at a value below fair-market value, which the IRS viewed as a violation of the rules. The requirement to list any transaction that essentially appears similar to the particulars of Notice 2004-8 should not be taken lightly because the penalty for failure to "list" or report such a transaction to the IRS, even if it is not considered a prohibited transaction, is $100,000!

Be careful of subtle self-dealing

An estate planning attorney whom I am familiar with decided to ask the Department of Labor to evaluate a transaction that one of her clients was contemplating, to see if they viewed the transaction as prohibited under IRC 4975. Essentially, two IRA shareholders (Messrs. B and R) are to invest in an LLC, which is considered a real estate operating company (REOC) because its purpose is to buy land, build a warehouse, and lease the warehouse to an S corporation, (of which Mr. B and Mr. G each own

50% making it a disqualified person in relation to Mr. B's IRA. The LLC's ownership is as follows:

- 49% owned by Mr. B's IRA;

- 31% owned by Mr. R's IRA ; and

- 20% owned by a Mr. G (who is also a 32% owner (personally) of the S corporation along with 68% ownership by Mr. B and his wife as community property).

According to the plan asset rules discussed earlier, because the LLC is a real estate operating company, its assets are not considered plan assets as a result of Mr. G's (who is not a disqualified person in relation to Mr. B and Mr. R) ownership and that of two unrelated IRAs. Therefore, because the entity's assets are not plan assets of any IRA, a transaction between the LLC and a disqualified person (the S corporation) should not be a prohibited transaction (the formula: plan + disqualified person + transaction = prohibited transaction, does not exist). To help clarify, the S corporation is a disqualified person in relation to Mr. B's IRA because it is 50% owned by him and his wife. For that reason, if the LLC was entirely owned by Mr. B's IRA, there would be a clear violation of IRC 4975.

So what is the problem, since we know that the LLC is not tantamount to Mr. B's IRA because the LLC's assets are not considered plan assets of any IRA? What rule was to be broken from the DOL's view? The DOL's analysis was based on an ERISA anti-abuse regulation (29CR 2509.75-2(a)). This regulation explains that a transaction between a disqualified person, such as the S corporation in this case, and an IRA, through an entity (the LLC) that does not have plan assets, is generally not considered a prohibited transaction. However, the regulation states that when a plan (Mr. B's IRA) invests in an entity for the purpose of having that entity engage in a transaction with a disqualified person (the S corporation), on a prearranged basis, then that is tantamount to a prohibited transaction.

Specifically, because of the leasing of the warehouse, the violation is the use by, or for the benefit of, a disqualified person of plan assets (in this case Mr. B). The DOL also stated that this may be self-dealing as well by virtue of Mr. B, as a disqualified person as fiduciary of his IRA, engaging in a prohibited self-dealing transaction (using his IRA to purchase property to be leased by a corporation that he holds a 50% interest in).

What is the lesson to be learned from DOL 2006-1A? That the understanding of whether or not a prohibited transaction is being created when your IRA invests can be daunting? Possibly, but let's change this scenario a little to try to simplify things in your mind. Assume the same ownership in the LLC, but now assume that neither Mr. B nor his wife has an interest in the S corporation. Do you think that a prohibited transaction would occur if the LLC leased the warehouse to the S corporation?

Assuming there are no other facts in the scenario that would give rise to the possibility of a prohibited transaction, then no, there would be no prohibited transaction. Now suppose Mr. B's wife had a 49% or less interest in the S corporation (and Mr. B had none) and the LLC's ownership remained as well; would this be problematic? Analyzing this question can be a little complex. First, the S corporation would not be a disqualified person under 4975, and, therefore, on its own, the transaction with the LLC would not be considered prohibited, unless the DOL determines that the transaction Mr. B engaged in as the fiduciary of his IRA was intentionally designed to gain a personal benefit through his relationship with his wife, a large shareholder of the S corporation. It is quite possible that proper legal counsel could set up a structure and process to establish that self-dealing was not occurring in this example.

The moral to this story, however, is that when you look through all the entities your IRA may invest in, and you see yourself or another disqualified person (such as your daughter) benefiting from your IRA's transaction, it is at least time to consult a knowledgeable attorney before proceeding, or to abandon the transaction altogether. Otherwise, at the very least, you are playing Russian roulette with the DOL and IRS.

Some final words of advice

There are tremendous opportunities for wealth creation through self-directed IRAs without exposing your retirement plan to risk from attempting to have your "cake and eat it too." If you are knowingly attempting to obtain a personal benefit through your IRA's investment, my advice is to stop right there. There are no legitimate workarounds. If it looks like a duck, walks like a duck, and quacks like a duck, it's a duck!

The Don'ts

1. Don't create a prohibited transaction by having your IRA transact with yourself personally, your spouse, descendents, or ascendants (e.g., avoid self-dealing);

2. Don't engage in a transaction with your IRA and a third party's IRA on a "quid pro quo" or reciprocal basis in attempt to circumvent an otherwise prohibited transaction;

3. Don't deal with an entity that you or the sum of your related disqualified persons own 50% or more of with your retirement account;

4. Don't personally guarantee a loan that your IRA obtains;

5. Don't make personal (including disqualified persons) use of any asset your IRA owns;

6. Don't provide more than ministerial services (e.g., decision making) to your IRA or IRA-owned entity (e.g., no "sweat equity");

7. Don't take any personal compensation for any services provided to your IRA or as a result of a transaction that your IRA participates in;

8. Don't engage in any transaction that results in any personal gain (e.g., a guarantee of employment) for you or your disqualified persons (other than the benefit that your IRA receives);

9. Don't co-invest personally with your IRA in any asset that you use as loan collateral; and

10. Don't take constructive receipt of any income from assets owned by your IRA and do not pay (personally) the expenses of assets held by your IRA.

The Do's

1. Do consider including alternative assets in your retirement portfolio for diversification and risk protection;

2. Do consult with a knowledgeable advisor when in doubt.

3. Do educate yourself. Read all the free educational material available on our website and referenced in this book and in the book *IRA Wealth* by Pat Rice;

4. Do find out how you can accelerate earnings on real estate through leverage.

5. Do consider the possibility of using an IRA when you, a relative or friend starts a new business.

6. Do consider your Roth IRA for those investments with the greatest upside potential;

7. Do maximize your contributions to 401(k)s that are matched by your employer and contribute to Roth IRAs each year, if eligible;

8. Do, if you are a financial services professional, consider learning more about self-directed IRAs as a means to stay at the forefront of the knowledge curve and to become the "go to" self-directed IRA expert in your area;

9. Do tell your friends about the possibilities of self-directed IRAs—they'll thank you; and

10. Do consider getting your children started on saving for retirement and education while they are young by establishing a Roth IRA or Coverdell Education Savings Account.

CHAPTER 10

Prohibited Transactions Quiz

Tom Anderson

Now that you've read all about prohibited transactions, you're ready to test your knowledge so that you're prepared when you start investing with your self-directed IRA or retirement account. After all, would a father give his teenage son, just turned 16, the keys to his new Ferrari, before he knew that his son was capable of driving?

The following selected questions have been posed to PENSCO Trust over a number of years. They appear just as we received them from investors or their professionals, with the exception of spelling corrections. The answers immediately follow each question, so don't peek!

Not all answers are Yes ("Y"—you can do as outlined based on the facts presented without creating a prohibited transaction) or No ("N"—you cannot because a prohibited transaction is involved); some are dependent on additional information not provided in the question. For these, check "M" (for maybe) and add any assumptions or caveats with your answer in the space provided. You can check your score based on the number of questions you answered correctly. Good luck and have fun!

1) Q. I'm self-employed and have about $90k to invest in a new LLC I am forming to purchase investment real estate. The land will cost $400,000 and will be funded by my own savings, the $90k, and my brother's self-directed IRA.

Y   N   M   _____

_____

_____

A) YES or Maybe are acceptable, as this would not constitute a prohibited transaction, provided that the IRA funds were not essential to make the transaction work for the IRA owner (e.g., he or she had other financial resources that could have been deployed, but he or she decided to use the IRA's resources as it appeared to be a good investment for the IRA).

2.) Q. Will self-directed IRA products allow me to purchase shares of stock in a small business that I own as well as real estate?

Y   N   M   _____

A) No, if you own a company (50% or more ownership, you cannot have your IRA invest in it).

3.) Q. We are interested in the possibility of investing our IRA funds in a real estate franchise we have bought with our son. We have formed an S corporation. Please advise.

Y   N   M   _____

_____

_____

A) This is easy: NO. You can't invest an IRA in an S corporation. Furthermore, because they already own this franchise, they are disqualified persons. In addition to the S problem, they would be creating a Prohibited Transaction (PT).

4.) Q. I want to open a self-directed Roth account and fund an LLC with IRA funds. Can I add more IRA funds to the LLC later? Can I be the manager of the LLC without risking prohibited transaction? To take a distribution, would the LLC need to send funds back to PENSCO, or could I write my own check from the LLC?

Y   N   M   _____

_____

_____

A) The answer is YES. First, he can fully fund the company with his IRA. Second, there is an exemption to allow an IRA to put more funds into an entity that it owns 100% of, although ironically, if it owned 90%, for example, through an initial investment, it could not add more funds through the IRA. Yes, he can manage the entity; however, he would be well-advised to have a knowledgeable CPA or attorney review the formative documentation for the entity and then review each transaction before execution to be sure it won't be considered prohibited and provided he receives no compensation and only performs ministerial services for the LLC. And, yes, if there are any distributions, they have to go to the IRA and not to the IRA owner.

5.) Q. I am a certified financial planner who has a number of clients interested in making some real estate investments within their IRA accounts. A client would like to do some very specific real estate refurbishing through his son's LLC with IRA money. Reading through all the rules and regulations I quickly realized that we were going to need some help to get this IRA structured correctly!

Y   N   M   _____

A) NO, it appears that the person's IRA would be investing in his son's (owned) LLC for the purchase of conducting a refurbishing business. Assuming the son owns 50% or more of the LLC, the IRA cannot invest in it.

6.) Q. Two partners and I are looking at purchasing property using a real estate IRA. Do we have to use a management company to collect rent? One of the partners owns his own construction company; is his company allowed to do the work on the property?

Y   N   M   _____

_____

_____

A) NO, the partner cannot use his construction company to do work on property his IRA is invested in. In addition, the function of rent collection is definitely in the gray area, because that is a function normally performed for a fee by professional firms and, therefore, would probably not be interpreted as ministerial if examined in an audit. If you're using leverage (an IRA non-recourse loan), your lender may require the use of a property manager unless you have previous experience with rental properties.

7.) Q. My son is getting ready to purchase his first home. I would like to use some of my IRA money for his down payment as a way of obtaining more real estate in my portfolio. Is it possible to do that with a self-directed IRA? What is the process, and how long would it take before I have the money available to close?

Y   N   M   _____

_____

_____

A) NO. He cannot make the down payment on his son's first home. The closing process, assuming his IRA is set up with a self-directed custodian and he was engaging in a permitted investment, will take no longer than a closing performed with taxable funds.

8.) Q. I am terminating my medical corporation profit-sharing plan and will roll over to an IRA. I have two separate limited-partner shares in real estate buildings that have long-term leases. What is the process for rolling these assets into a self-directed IRA?

Y   N   M   _____

_____

_____

A) YES, this individual can roll these investments over in kind or as is without having to liquidate them. The process entails having him or her as trustee contact the sponsor of the Limited Partnerships to advise them to change the registration (ownership) from his pension plan to his IRA and to notify the receiving IRA custodian, who will then work with the trustee and asset sponsor to effect the rollover.

9.) Q. I currently have several IRAs for my wife, me, and our children. The company I am with is reluctant to let me invest them in an LLC where I am the managing member. I would like to put this money in rental real estate, and I own a property management firm which is a sub S corporation.

Y   N   M   _____

_____

A) NO. The reluctance is well-founded, because the intention is to use a company he owns to provide services to an entity to be owned by the IRAs of disqualified persons.

10.) Q. I want to buy residential real property in Jerusalem, which would be managed by a property management firm in Jerusalem. It would be rented to any qualified person. Can you tell me if you will administer an IRA that I would rollover to you from the current trustee for this purpose?

Y   N   M   _____

_____

A) YES. This transaction is permitted and does not appear to pose the potential for a prohibited transaction. However, the logistics, once known, may make the administration difficult or impractical, so more would need to be known about the mechanics. But, again, this does not appear to be prohibited just because the real estate is outside of the United States. It will be difficult to find non-recourse financing if you can't purchase the property outright.

11.) Q. I want to use some of my IRA funds to buy an ownership interest in a real estate franchise. At a certain point, all of the owners will divide the profits. Also, I will be working for this company as a real estate agent and would be earning commissions and paying my own business costs. You do not have to be a part owner to be an agent, but at this time all owners will be working agents. Does this sound acceptable?

Y   N   M   _____

A) NO. This appears to be self-dealing, as his funds would enable him to earn commissions, and the structure indicates that all franchisee member owners are enabling themselves to receive income personally from their investments.

12.) Q. Can I invest in mobile homes (without real estate) in an IRA? If I'm fixing up real estate or mobile homes and selling them (without renting), how hard will the paperwork and administration be? Will I need to fill out forms and get permission every time I need a bucket of paint?

Y   N   M   _____

_____

_____

A) YES, he or she can purchase these and pay some third party to fix them up before reselling. He cannot pay these expenses personally, but he can submit bills to the custodian, who will pay the vendors from funds in the IRA. Alternatively, he could employ a third party to maintain the books and bank account associated with income and expense to facilitate payments as long as regular reports of the balance and activity of the account are submitted to the custodian.

13.) Q. I am interested in using IRA funds to hold loans on manufactured homes that are placed on rented spaces or buying single-family homes. I'm over 59½ years old; none of my funds are in a Roth IRA. Is this OK?

Y   N   M   _____

_____

_____

A) YES. Assuming the land is not owned by the IRA investor, there does not appear to be any PT involved with this scenario. One thing to keep in mind, however, is that frequent execution of this scenario may constitute running a development business, therefore making the IRA subject to UBIT because it is running a trade or business.

14.) Q. I own a business (LLC) that is leasing space for its use. I have formed another LLC to purchase new space with the intent of leasing it back to first LLC. Can I invest in a real estate IRA and then lease the space back to my business LLC?

Y   N   M   _____

_____

A) NO. No explanation necessary. This is a "step" or "linked" transaction, intended to avoid an otherwise prohibited transaction and, therefore, would be treated as a prohibited transaction.

15.) Q. My wife and I own a condo, and since the market is slow right now, I want to design a plan where I could transfer ownership to an LLC in which my self-directed IRA is the sole shareholder.

Y   N   M   _____

_____

A) NO. You would be creating a prohibited transaction, as this appears to be a preconceived self-dealing scheme much like 2006-1A.

16.) Q. Can we purchase in the U.S. Virgin Islands or foreign property? I was told it cannot be our prime source of income, and we have to "live there" for at least two weeks out of the year.

Y   N   M   _____

A) NO. In fact, you cannot live there at all. As to the prime source of income, the answer is unclear, because there is no limit as to how much an IRA (which is treated as a separate legal entity) can earn, and the amount it earns from investments it holds has no relationship to the amount the IRA owner earns.

17.) Q. I am about to purchase water-front land adjacent to my second home from an unrelated third party. I would be pleased to use IRA funds for the purchase. I would like to structure the deal to allow the possibility of building a retirement house on the land and making it a primary residence.

Y   N   M   _____
_____
_____
_____

A) NO. The individual cannot (without tax and possibly penalty consequences) build a retirement home with his IRA and move into it. Also, there are potential self-dealing implications about the IRA property being adjacent to his current residence. For example, is he trying to preserve a view? Will he park his car on the IRA property?

18.) Q. I am interested in purchasing undeveloped land in Panama. I would just hold it for three to five years and then sell it. My CPA says I can borrow against my IRA to do this. The IRA wouldn't own the real estate; I would just borrow money from the IRA. She says I need to put the IRA funds into a self-directed account. Is this something I can do?

Y   N   M   _____
_____
_____

A) NO. CPA or not, your IRA cannot lend you money. Otherwise your IRA could purchase undeveloped property in Panama.

19.) Q. I am purchasing an investment condo and would like to put it in a self-directed IRA. The contract is signed, and the closing date is August 18. Can I simply establish an IRA with you folks and place this purchase in it?

Y   N   M   _____
_____
_____

A) NO. You cannot transfer the right (contract) that you enter into personally to your IRA. You could cancel that contract and enter into a new contract with your IRA as the purchaser if the seller agrees.

Are you ready to see how you did? If you didn't respond properly to whether or not the transaction would be permitted for a self-directed IRA, don't count that answer as correct. Add up all your correct answers when you are done assessing your responses. A score of 17 or more correct is exceptional, 16 or more excellent, and 14 or more is very good; 12 is good, and 10 is fair. If you had fewer than 10 correct, go back and reread the last chapter.

I hope that you now are aware of what you can safely do to build wealth through a self-directed IRA. To summarize, there are three assets types that you cannot purchase. Remember them? Collectibles, life insurance, and the stock of a subchapter S corporation. And there are certain transactions that can create prohibited transactions. Generally, these involve "disqualified persons" or self-dealing. That being said, I recommend that you discuss your scenario with your custodian or a knowledgeable advisor when in doubt, just in case!

The content in chapters 9 and 10 are the opinion of the author and do not necessarily represent the opinions and views of his employer and do not represent legal, tax or investment advice in any form. Readers are advised to consult with their own professional advisors before acting on the information provided.

CHAPTER 11

Frequently Asked Questions

1. Why is it hard to find a non-recourse loan?

Non-recourse loans for IRAs are highly specialized and require an expertise that most lenders do not have or want to have. Because non-recourse loans cater to the world of IRAs, the legal and reporting requirements are above the level of knowledge for the average financial institution. NASB offers non-recourse loans in every state because it is highly specialized with tremendous experience in the area of real estate transactions within IRAs.

2. Are there alternatives to a commercial non-recourse loan?

No; if an IRA is to use debt financing, it must be a non-recourse loan. Publication 590 (www.irs.gov) states that an IRA cannot be used as "security for a loan." The only option to satisfy this restriction is using a non-recourse lender such as NASB or a hard money/private lender.

3. Can I purchase real estate with other investors?

Yes, you can divide ownership between your retirement account, other investors' personal funds, and other IRA accounts. Let's say that your IRA owns 50% of the property and your friend's IRA owns the other 50% on a $100,000 single-family home purchase. Each IRA is required to make a down payment of $25,000 for this particular transaction.

4. Am I required to use a property manager?

Not necessarily. The rules allow you to perform ministerial services for your IRA and IRA investments. The selection of a rental tenant and the passing along of rent checks and expense invoices to the custodian are generally permitted. However, providing improvements or repairs through your own labor or that of a disqualified person would constitute a prohibited transaction. This type of sweat equity (e.g., repairing the roof of your IRA-owned property yourself) is not permitted. Hiring someone who is not related to you is permitted, however, as long as you don't pay the expenses yourself. You should send the invoice to your custodian who will then make the payment from your IRA.

5. What happens when I sell the property I own in my IRA? Taxable event?

When the property is sold, and if the property has had debt attached to it in the last 12 months from the date of sale, a tax on the sale could potentially be owed, just as in a non-IRA transaction. If the property was held longer than 12 months, any gain would receive capital gains (15%) treatment, but only on the portion of the gain that was still debt financed.

For example, if the property generated a long-term capital gain of $100,000 (amount realized less adjusted basis), this gain would be reduced by the debt/cost basis ratio remaining on the property. (For this calculation only, the debt/cost ratio is the highest ratio over the prior 12 months before the sale.) If the highest debt/cost ratio over the prior 12 months was 35%, then the $100,000 of long-term capital gain would be multiplied by 35% to reduce the gain to $35,000. This $35,000 gain would be taxed at the long-term capital gains rate (which is currently 15%). This would result in the IRA owing capital gain taxes on sale of $5,250 ($35,000 ×15%).

As an aside, if, when the property was sold, there was no debt on the property over the prior 12 months, then there would be no capital gain tax owed. The capital gain tax calculation computed above is only a result of debt being owed on the property within 12 months of sale.

6. Can I live on the property I own in my IRA?

No, you can neither live on the property, nor use it for any personal benefit, including parking your car on the property because it would trigger a prohibited transaction.

7. Can I buy real estate in my LLC that is funded by my IRA?

Yes, a list of IRA LLC facilitators is included in the back of the book. You will need to create an LLC in which your IRA purchases shares of the LLC. Title is taken in the name of the LLC and not the IRA.

8. Will a non-recourse loan show up on my credit report under my Social Security number?

No, it will go under the Tax ID number of your self-directed IRA custodian/administrator or the entity buying the property (i.e., LLC, Solo-K, Partnership). This is good news for investors who have multiple investment properties and may be limited to the number of investment properties they can own in their personal name and still qualify for conforming loans.

9. Who is North American Savings Bank?

NASB is a Federal Savings Bank that was founded in 1927. They're publicly traded under the ticker symbol NASB and are federally regulated and supervised by the OTS (Office of Thrift Supervision, Division of Department of Treasury). www.nasb.com

10. What is UBIT/UDFI?

Unrelated business income tax and unrelated debt-financed income are concepts that sometimes subject IRAs and other "tax-exempt" entities to taxation on certain types of activities. The unrelated business income tax is technically a tax on income that a tax-exempt entity generates that is "unrelated" to its tax-exempt purpose. If your IRA owned and operated a coffee shop, that "trade or business" income is subject to tax just as a coffee shop owned by non-IRA funds would be.

Unrelated debt-financed income is a subset of the unrelated business income tax. This tax is based on the leveraged portion of taxable income that a property generates. What is important to note here is that for this UDFI calculation, the calculation includes the same deductible items that a non-IRA owner of real estate would include in his/her computation of taxable income. So items like depreciation, interest expense, real estate taxes, etc., are included in the UDFI computation. If the end result is a negative taxable income number, then no UDFI is owed.

11. Why will a non-recourse lender typically lend up to 70% LTV? Is this an IRS or lender requirement?

This is a lender requirement to reduce the level of risk. Because there is no-recourse against the individual borrower (IRA account holder), a lender will protect itself by requiring more money down because the lender's only recourse for repayment of loan default is to foreclose and sell the real estate.

12. If you use leverage to purchase real estate, who makes the monthly mortgage payments?

The self-directed IRA that purchases the property is required to make the monthly mortgage payment. You cannot use your personal funds because this would be considered co-mingling.

13. Will North American Savings Bank lend non-recourse to other entities other than a self-directed IRA?

Yes, NASB will lend directly to IRAs or LLCs, profit-sharing plans, solo K plans, partnerships, and C corporations that are owned by a retirement plan.

14. Is there a limit to how many properties I can purchase in my IRA?

No, an IRA can purchase unlimited properties.

15. Can I pay for repairs/improvements on a property that I own in my IRA with my personal funds?

No, all funds must come from the self-directed IRA that purchased the property.

16. Why does a non-recourse lender require reserves in the retirement account?

This takes into account any adjustments in real estate taxes or property hazard insurance rates, as well as any potential repairs to the property. If a repair needed to be made and there were no reserves, the account holder would invoke a prohibited transaction to make those repairs by using personal (non-IRA) funds. Also, if the account holder loses a tenant and is no longer collecting rent each month, the monthly payments must be made from the IRA reserves.

17. Why does North American Savings Bank escrow for taxes and insurance?

The IRS requires all expenses to come from the IRA. This includes property taxes and homeowner's insurance. In a scenario with only 30% down, the lender is the primary investor and wants to make sure all taxes and insurance are current.

18. What is debt service coverage ratio (DSCR) and how is it used?

Because these properties are investment properties and the property and leases are the only security for the non-recourse loan, there are some income requirements for the rental properties imposed by the lender. The financed property must generate sufficient net operating income (NOI) to exceed the debt service mortgage payments. For single-family homes this can be 15–25% positive cash flow with sufficient IRA reserves. Properties that have two to four units should have a Net Operating Income of 20–25%.

Debt Service Coverage Ratio Example
$200,000 property (single family home) with a
$100,000 IRA non-recourse loan

Gross Annual Income (GAI):

Rent ($1,400/month × 12) $16,800

Costs:

Vacancy (7% × GAI)	$-1,176
Taxes	$-2,500
Insurance	$-800
Maintenance ($420/unit)	$-420
Management Fee (6% × GAI)	$-1,008

Net Operating Income (NOI) $10,896

Annualized Principal and Interest payments equal $8,482, based on a $100,000 loan at 7% for 25 years.

Formula for Debt Service Coverage Ratio:
Net Operating Income/Annual P&I = Debt Service Coverage Ratio

$10,896/$8,482= 1.28 DSCR

In this example, 1.0 is breakeven and anything above 1.0 is positive cash flow which is deposited into the IRA.

19. How much can I contribute to my IRA every year?

As of 2010 you can contribute $5,000 per IRA accountholder and $6,000 if you're over the age of 50.

20. Can I use my IRA to lend to others?

Yes, as long as the person is not a disqualified person and the money isn't used to fund an operation in which you have any ownership or financial interest. Please check with a qualified tax advisor before engaging in this type of loan activity.

21. What happens if the property I own in my IRA goes into foreclosure?

First, you need to know that you do have the ability to loan money to your IRA (your personal funds) in order to sustain its operation and/or the viability of any assets it already owns under DOL PTE 80-26. The loan must be interest free and be documented within 60 days of being funded by a note payable to you by your IRA. There is no specific maturity date requirement or limit to the size of the loan as long as it is being used to support your existing IRA and its investments (e.g., not being used to purchase a new asset). If you are behind in your mortgage payments, and you've lost your tenant, you can make up the difference by lending money to your IRA.

If you are unable to loan money to your IRA, and your bank forecloses on your IRA-owned property, your IRA will lose the property to the bank. However, because the loan was a non-recourse loan (See chapter 4), your IRA will retain any other assets in your IRA and you will not be personally liable for any portion of the debt (that includes your credit rating).

22. Does the IRS require an appraisal every year to determine the value of the property? What is the cost?

Custodians are required to report the fair market value (FMV) of assets at the end of each year to their customers and the IRS. Generally speaking, it is industry practice to acquire valuations of illiquid (nontraded) assets such as real estate on a "best efforts" basis from the asset sponsor or IRA owner. Most custodians will accept the opinion of a licensed real estate broker based on recent comparables with similar properties for those years where there is not a taxable event (e.g., an IRA distribution). Whenever there is a taxable event, such as when minimum distributions commence at age 70.5, the custodians will require a full appraisal from a qualified professional. Although costs vary by locale, generally, depending on the nature and size of the property (e.g., residential, commercial, industrial), such appraisals will cost between $400 and $2,000.

23. Can I buy real estate outside the United States?

Yes, but most likely, you need to pay all cash or use a private lender because there are currently no U.S.-based banks providing non-recourse loans to IRAs to purchase property in foreign countries. You will also need to find an IRA that permits foreign real estate investment and is familiar with doing so. Generally, each country has its own rules, and some countries do not recognize an IRA as a legal entity capable of holding title to real estate. In other cases, foreigners cannot own real estate in certain countries (e.g., India).

One thing to keep in mind is that the process of acquiring foreign property can be more protracted and involved than purchasing property in the United States. Besides legal issues, which may have to be researched, there are translation and currency issues, etc. One important consideration when purchasing in another country is the effect of exchange rates on your return. If the exchange rate (the rate by which you can exchange the proceeds in a foreign currency to U.S. dollars and vice versa) declines, you may negate any gains in capital appreciation from the sale. On the other hand, it can work in your favor if the value of the U.S. dollar increases against the foreign currency between the time you purchase and the time you sell. Some savvy investors have more than doubled their money due to the effect that the exchange rate had on their real estate investment.

GLOSSARY

#

990-T Tax Form—A form filed with the IRS for a tax-exempt organization or retirement plan that has $1,000 or more in gross income from an unrelated business must file Form 990-T. This form applies to a retirement plan that utilizes leverage (non-recourse loan). The due date for this tax return is the 15th day of the fourth month following the end of the tax year. The form can be found at www.irs.gov/pub/irs-pdf/f990t.pdf

1099-R Tax Form—A form filed with the IRS which reports distributions from pensions, annuities, retirement plans, IRAs, or insurance contracts and capital gains and/or dividends from its issuer.

5498 Tax Form—A form filed annually with the IRS which reports the amount of IRA contributions and the fair market value of the IRA.

401(k) Plan—A type of defined contribution pension plan provided by many corporations for their employees. The plans allow employees to set aside a percentage of their pretax salaries into an investment account which can grow tax deferred until retirement age. Most corporate 401(k) plans allow the employee to manage their investment choices from a specified list of fund options.

403(b) Plan—A retirement plan similar to a 401(k) plan offered by nonprofit organizations, such as universities and some charitable organizations, rather than corporations.

A

Abstract or Title Search—The process of reviewing all transactions that have been recorded in order to determine whether any defects in the title exist that could interfere with a clear property ownership transfer.

Active Participant—An individual who benefited from a qualified retirement plan, or a qualified self-employed retirement plan, even if only for one day during the year.

Additional Principal Payment—Additional money paid to the lender, apart from the scheduled loan payments, to pay more of the principal balance, shortening the length of the loan.

Adjustable Rate Mortgage (ARM)—A home loan with an interest rate that is adjusted periodically.

Adjusted Gross Income (AGI)—Gross, or total, income from taxable sources minus certain deductions. Income includes wages, interest and dividends, and long- and short-term capital gains and losses. Deductions may include unreimbursed business and medical expenses, contributions to a deductible individual retirement account (IRA), and alimony.

Amortization Schedule—A chart or table that shows the percentage of each payment that will be applied toward principal and interest over the life of the mortgage and how the loan balance decreases until it reaches a zero balance.

Amortization Term—The number of months it will take to repay the loan based on a predefined scheduled payment.

Annual Contribution Limits—The dollar amount that the IRS allows you to contribute each year to an IRA. The 2010 annual contribution limits for traditional and Roth IRAs is $5,000 for individuals under age 50 and $6,000 for individuals age 50 and older.

Appraisal—The estimated value of a property on a particular date given by a professional appraiser, usually presented in a written document.

Appraiser—A certified individual who is qualified by education, training, and experience to estimate the value of real and personal property.

Appreciation—An increase in the home's or property's value.

Assessed Value—The value placed on a home that is determined by a tax assessor in order to calculate a tax base.

Assessor—A public officer who evaluates property value for the purpose of taxation.

B

Balloon Loan—A mortgage in which the monthly payments are not large enough to repay the loan by the end of the term, and the final payment is one large payment for the remaining balance.

Base Loan Amount—The amount that forms the basis for the loan payments.

Blanket Mortgage—A loan used to finance the purchase of two or more pieces of real estate.

Bridge Loan—A short-term loan secured by real estate that provides interim financing for the purchase of new property until the existing property can be sold.

Buydown Mortgage—A home loan option in which the borrower pays points to buy down the interest to a lower rate.

C

Capital Gain—The amount by which an asset's selling price exceeds its initial purchase price.

Carry-back Financing—A type of funding in which the seller agrees to finance a portion of the sales price by accepting a secured note from the buyer for the seller's financing.

Carry-back Contribution—A contribution made to a Roth or traditional IRA between January 1 and April 15 for the prior tax year.

Cash Flow—The amount of income an investor receives for a rental property after all expenses and loan payments are deducted.

Catch-up Contribution—An additional contribution available for individuals age 50 and older. The IRA catch-up contribution limit for 2010 is $1,000 above the $5,000 limit.

Certificate of Occupancy—A written document issued by a local government or building department certifying that a home or building is suitable for occupancy.

Clear Title—A property title that is free of liens, defects, or other legal encumbrances.

Closing—Date on which the title to a property is conveyed to its buyer and the sales proceeds are transferred to its seller.

Closing Costs—All costs and expenses paid by the buyer and seller related to the sale of real estate including loan fees, title insurance, prepaid escrows, and appraisal fees.

Co-mingling—Combining funds from different accounts for the purchase of an investment.

Collateral—Assets pledged by a borrower to secure a loan or other credit and subject to seizure in the event of default.

Compensation—Income received from base salary, commissions, bonuses, overtime, and vacation pay. Self-employed individuals use their net earnings when determining their compensation.

Condominium—A type of ownership in which all of the unit owners own the common areas and buildings jointly and have sole ownership in the unit to which they hold the title.

Condominium Hotel—A condominium project that involves registration desks, short-term occupancy, food, and cleaning services and is generally operated as a commercial hotel while the units are individually owned.

Construction Loan—A short-term loan to finance the cost of construction, usually dispensed in stages to the builder throughout the construction project.

Construction-to-Permanent Loan—A construction loan that can be converted to long-term financing after the construction is complete.

Contingent Beneficiary—The individual(s) or entity(ies) designated to receive retirement account proceeds if the primary beneficiary(ies) are deceased.

Contribution—The amount contributed to a Roth IRA or Traditional IRA for a particular tax year. Contributions (other than rollover contributions) must be made in cash or check and are subject to annual contribution limits.

Contributory IRA—An IRA that is funded by cash contributions by the IRA owner and not rolled over from another retirement plan or IRA.

Conventional Loan—A loan not guaranteed or insured by the federal government.

Conversion—The changing of a traditional IRA, SEP, or other IRA funded with pretax funds to a Roth IRA. A conversion is considered a taxable event according to the IRS.

Conveyance—The transferring of a property title from one individual to another.

Cooperative—Also called a co-op. A type of common property ownership by multiple residents of a multiunit housing complex. Residents own shares in the cooperative corporation that owns the property, thereby having the right to occupy a specific apartment or unit.

Coverdell Educational Savings Account—Also known as an Education IRA or Education Savings Account. A savings account that allows parents, grandparents, and others to contribute cumulatively for the education expenses of a child. Contributions are not tax deductible, but withdrawals are tax free if used for qualified expenses such as tuition and room and board. The designated beneficiary must be under the age of 18 when the contribution is made. Coverdell account contributions don't count against an individual's annual contribution limit for individual IRAs.

Cross-Collateralization—A grouping of mortgages or properties that jointly secure one debt obligation.

D

Debt Service Coverage Ratio (DSCR)—A measurement of a property's ability to generate enough revenue to cover the cost of its mortgage payments and expenses. The property's annual net operating income divided by all expenses including the mortgage.

Deed—A legal document that conveys property ownership to the buyer.

Deed in Lieu of Foreclosure—A deed given to the lender in order to satisfy the mortgage debt owed by the borrower to avoid a foreclosure.

Deed of Trust—A security instrument provided by a borrower to a lender that allows a lender to foreclose on a property in the event that the borrower defaults on the loan.

Default—This occurs when a borrower fails to fulfill a duty to take care of an obligation, such as making monthly mortgage payments.

Defined Benefit Plan—A company retirement plan in which the employee receives a specific amount based on the salary history and years of service. This is also called a pension plan.

Defined Contribution Plan—A company retirement plan in which the employee elects to defer a portion of income into an investment vehicle provided by the employer.

A 401(k) and 403(b) are examples of this type of plan.

Depreciation—A decrease or loss in value of real estate because of age, wear, or market conditions. Also an accounting term to describe the method of attributing the historical or purchase cost of an asset across its use full life.

Direct Rollover—A distribution from a qualified pension plan, such as a 401(k) plan or 403(b) plan that is sent directly to the trustee, custodian, or issuer of the receiving IRA. This is reported to the IRS as a rollover. This can only be done once per year, per account.

Discount Points—Fees that a lender charges in order to provide a lower interest rate.

Distribution—Any withdrawal of cash or assets from an IRA account or retirement plan.

Diversification—A strategy used to minimize the exposure of risk by investing in different asset classes.

Down Payment—The variance between the purchase price and the portion provided by the lender in the form of a mortgage.

Due Diligence—The process of investigation performed by a real estate investor to confirm that the property is as represented by the seller.

Due on Sale Clause—The language in a security instrument (mortgage) that states that the full balance of the loan may be called due if the property is sold or there is transfer of ownership.

E

Early Distribution—Distributions taken from a traditional or Roth IRA before age 59½. Early distributions are subject to a 10% early distribution penalty unless an exception applies.

Earnest Money—The funds a buyer provides when making an offer to purchase a piece of real estate.

Encroachment—The act of improving or upgrading that illegally intrudes onto another party's property.

Encumbrance—A claim or liability against a property.

End Loan—Converting a construction loan to a permanent financing loan once the construction is complete.

Equity—The value of a property after existing liabilities (i.e., loans) have been deducted.

Employee Retirement Income Security Act of 1974 (ERISA)—This is the labor law covering qualified plans and incorporates both the pertinent Internal Revenue Code provisions by reference and labor law provisions.

Excess Contribution—The amount an IRA contribution exceeds the allowable limits, on which the IRS applies a penalty. A 6% excise (penalty) tax applies on the excess contribution each year until corrected.

Escrow Account—An account established by a mortgage lender or servicing company for the purpose of holding funds for the payment of items such as real estate taxes and homeowner's insurance.

Escrow Company—A neutral company that acts as third party to help facilitate and ensure all conditions are met for the closing of real estate transactions.

F

Fair Market Value—The highest price that a buyer is willing to pay and the lowest a seller is willing to accept. The fair market value of IRA assets is reported to each IRA holder and the IRS each year. The December 31 fair market values are used for reporting purposes.

Federal Home Loan Mortgage Corporation (FHLMC)—Also known as Freddie Mac. A company that purchases mortgages from lenders and resells them as securities in the secondary market.

Federal Housing Administration (FHA)—A part of the U.S. Department of Housing and Urban Development (HUD). FHA provides mortgage insurance on single-family, multifamily, and manufactured homes made by the FHA-approved lenders throughout the United States and its territories.

Federal National Mortgage Association (FNMA)—Also known as Fannie Mae. A company that purchases mortgages from lenders and resells them as securities in the secondary market.

Fee Simple—Absolute ownership of the land. The owner has the right to use it and can sell or pass to another by will or inheritance. It is the most common way real estate is owned.

Fiduciary—An individual, corporation, or association holding assets for another party, often with the legal authority and duty to make decisions regarding financial matters on behalf of the other party.

Fixed Rate—An interest rate that does not change during the entire term of the loan.

Flood Certification—An inspection to determine whether or not a property is located in a known flood zone. A lender will order a flood certification for each property to determine if flood insurance must but be purchased by the purchaser.

Flood Insurance—Insurance that covers physical damage to a property caused by flood. Flood insurance is not covered in a standard homeowner's policy.

For Sale by Owner (FSBO)—Process of marketing and selling a property without the use of real estate agent. The owner of the property works directly with the buyer or buyer's agent.

Foreclosure—The legal process in which a lender takes ownership of the property, usually due to the homeowner not making timely monthly mortgage payments.

G

Good-faith Estimate—A residential mortgage lender or broker's form to disclose the estimated costs associated with closing a loan.

Government National Mortgage Association (GNMA)—Guarantees the investors the timely payment of principal and interest on mortgage backed securities (MBS) backed by federally insured or guaranteed loans—mainly loans by the Federal Housing Administration (FHA) or guaranteed by the Department of Veteran Affairs (VA).

Grant—To give or transfer an interest in a property by deed or other documented method.

Grantee—The person or party to whom a grant is given.

Grantor—The person or party who conveys the grant to the grantee.

Guarantor—The party who guarantees an obligation and has a legal duty to fulfill it.

Guaranty—A promise made on behalf of the borrower to repay the debt if the borrower fails to repay as agreed.

H

High-Rise—Any building generally taller than six stories in a suburban district or 25 stories in a business district.

Homeowner's Insurance—Also known as Hazard Insurance, Property Insurance, Home Insurance, or Fire Insurance. Insurance that provides coverage for personal liability and hazard insurance coverage for the dwelling. This is a lender requirement.

Home Inspection—An objective analysis of a home's structure and systems by a certified inspector.

Home Inspector—A certified professional who assesses the condition of electrical, heating, plumbing, and structural systems in houses and other residences.

Homeowner's Association (HOA)—A group that governs a community, condominium/townhome building, or neighborhood and enforces the covenants, conditions, and restrictions set by the developer.

Homeowner's Association Dues—Payments that are made to the homeowner's association to cover various amenities and services provided by the homeowner's association such as maintenance of common areas, hazard insurance, garbage, mowing, and snow removal.

HVAC—Heating, ventilating, and air-conditioning.

I

Impounds—Also referred to as an escrow account.

Indirect Rollover—A rollover to an IRA from another IRA or allowable retirement plan that doesn't go directly from the retirement plan to the IRA. The distributed amounts are first paid to the individual recipient before being deposited into the IRA. Completion date is usually 60 days from the date of the initial withdrawal.

Individual Retirement Account (IRA)—A tax-favored account for an individual that permits individuals to set aside money each year, with earnings tax deferred until withdrawals begin at age 59½ or later. IRAs can be established at a bank, mutual fund, or brokerage, or with a self-directed IRA custodian or administrator.

Inflation—The overall general upward movement of the dollar value of goods and services in an economy over a period of time.

Interest Rate—The percentage of annual interest charged for a loan.

Interest Rate Ceiling—The maximum interest rate a lender can charge for an adjustable rate mortgage. This is also called a lifetime cap.

Interest Rate Floor—The minimum interest rate a lender can charge for an adjustable rate mortgage.

J

Joint Tenancy—A type of ownership of real or personal property by two or more persons in which each owns an undivided interest in the property.

Jumbo Loan—A loan that exceeds the maximum size limit set forth by Fannie Mae and Freddie Mac.

L

Lease—A written agreement between a property owner and tenant that defines the payments and conditions under which the tenant may occupy the real estate.

Lease Option—An option for the homebuyer to rent the property with the option to purchase at a later date. Normally, a portion of the rental payments are applied toward the down payment when the property is purchased.

Leasehold—The right to hold or use property for a fixed amount of time. The buyer does not own the land as with a fee simple purchase.

Leverage—The use of a small initial investment, credit, or borrowed funds to gain a very high return in relation to one's investment, to control a much larger investment, or to reduce one's own liability for any loss.

Lien—A claim placed by a creditor on a piece of real estate or property, to ensure the payment of a debt.

Loan Origination Fee—A fee a lender charges to cover the costs related for processing the loan paid at closing.

Loan Servicing—The acts performed by a lending institution to collect and process loan payments during the life of a loan. This involves billing the borrower; collecting payments of principal, interest, and payments into an escrow/impound account; disbursing funds from the escrow account to pay real estate taxes and insurance premiums.

Loan-to-Value (LTV)—The ratio of the fair market value of an asset compared to the value of the loan that is financed.

M

Maturity Date—The date when the principal balance of the loan is due.

Mechanic's Lien—A lien against real property as security for the payment for materials, repairs, or improvements to real estate. A supplier of materials or a contractor may file a lien against the subject real estate to ensure payment for materials or services provided.

Mixed Use Property—A property that has both residential and commercial units.

Modern Portfolio Theory (MPT)—Introduced by Nobel Prize winner Harry Markowitz in the 1950s, modern portfolio theory emphasizes that investors may minimize market risk for an expected level of return by constructing a diversified portfolio.

Mortgage—A loan used to finance the purchase of real estate, typically with set terms.

Mortgagee—The financial institution that lends money to the borrower.

Mortgagor—The person who borrows money secured by real estate.

Multi-dwelling Units—Properties that provide separate housing units for more than one family; yet, they only secure a single mortgage.

N

Negative Amortization—Results when the scheduled payment for principal and interest is less than the actual interest due, resulting in an increase of the principal amount due as unpaid interest that is added to the outstanding loan balance.

Net Cash Flow—The amount of money remaining from the income of a property after all costs and expenses from the property have been paid.

Net Operating Income (NOI)—The effective gross income from a property minus all operating expenses.

Non-conforming Loan—Any loan that does not meet the qualifications to be purchased by Freddie Mac or Fannie Mae.

Non-recourse Loan—A loan in which 100% of the collateral is the real estate. The borrower does not sign a personal guaranty and there in no recourse against the borrower or his/her assets. This is the only type of loan the IRS allows with self-directed retirement plans.

Non-deductible Contribution—A contribution made to an IRA that is considered nondeductible due to restrictions or by choice. An income tax deduction is not taken for this contribution. To report nondeductible contributions, you must file Form 8606 with your tax return.

O

Operating Expense—The regular costs associated with operating and managing a piece of real estate.

P

Per Diem Interest—Interest that is accrued daily.

Permanent Loan—Also known as an "End Loan." A long-term loan used for the purchase of real estate. This type of loan is frequently used to pay off a construction loan after completion of the property.

PITI—Acronym for principal, interest, taxes, and insurance. The four components make up the mortgage payment paid to the lender.

Planned Unit Development (PUD)—A development project or subdivision with individually owned units plus common areas that are owned and maintained by homeowner's association.

Point—One percent of the loan amount charged by the lender as a fee.

Preapproval Letter—A letter provided by the lender confirming the amount that can be borrowed based on the information provided by the applicant.

Prepaid Expenses—Payments collected before they're due by the lender, such as real estate taxes and homeowner's insurance.

Prepayment Penalty—A penalty that may be charged by the lender if the loan is paid off before the scheduled date of maturity.

Prime Rate—The best interest rate charged to a lender's best customers, usually for a short-term loan.

Principal—The amount of money borrowed in a mortgage before interest is included.

Primary Beneficiary—The individual(s) or entity(ies) designated to receive retirement account proceeds if the retirement plan account holder is deceased.

Profit-Sharing Plan—A defined contribution plan under which the employer makes discretionary contributions on behalf of its employees. A participant's retirement benefits are based on the amount in his individual account at retirement.

Prohibited Transaction—An individual retirement account transaction forbidden by the Internal Revenue Code that will result in a penalty or loss of the IRA's tax benefits.

Purchase Agreement—A legal agreement between the buyer and seller defining the terms and conditions of the real estate transaction.

Q

Qualified Distribution (Roth IRA)—Distributions made from a Roth IRA that are tax and penalty free. In order to be a qualified distribution, the following two requirements must be met:

1. A withdrawal must occur at least five years after the Roth IRA owner established and funded the Roth IRA.

2. At least one of the following requirements must be met:

   a) The Roth IRA holder must be at least age 59½ when the distribution occurs.

   b) Used toward the purchase or rebuilding of a first home for the Roth IRA holder or a qualified family member.

   c) The distribution occurs after the Roth IRA holder becomes disabled.

   d) The assets are distributed to the beneficiary of the Roth IRA holder after the owner's death.

Qualified Retirement Plan—Any plan that qualifies for favorable tax treatment by meeting the requirements of the Internal Revenue Code.

Quitclaim Deed—A deed releasing all of a person's interest in a property or land.

R

Raw Land—A piece of real estate that is undeveloped and in its natural state.

Real Estate Investment Trust (REIT)—A corporation or trust that uses the pooled capital of multiple investors to purchase and manage real estate assets and/or mortgage loans.

Real Estate Owned (REO)—Property owned by a lender through a foreclosure.

Real Estate Settlement Procedures Act (RESPA)—This is the federal law that protects consumers from predatory lending practices by requiring lenders to disclose closing costs prior to collecting funds for processing the loan application, except a lender may collect a credit report fee before disclosing the closing costs. RESPA also prevents lenders from payment of kickbacks to real estate agents.

Real Property—Land and anything affixed to the land.

Rehab—Short for rehabilitation. Extensive renovation to improve a piece of real estate to extend the life of the property and increase the fair market value.

Rehab Mortgage—A short-term loan meant to fund the repairs and improvements for a home or building.

Required Beginning Date—The date the IRA account holder must take their first minimum required distribution. The date is usually April 1 after the IRA account holder turns 70½. This does not apply to Roth IRAs.

Required Minimum Distribution (RMD)—The minimum annual required distribution amount for an IRA holder who reaches age 70½. A simplified table established by the IRS is used to determine the distribution amount based on life expectancy and age.

Rollover—A tax-free transfer or deposit distributed from a qualified retirement plan into an IRA or other qualified plan within a specific time frame, usually 60 days.

Roth IRA—An IRA established in the Taxpayer Relief Act of 1997 which allows taxpayers, subject to certain income limits, to save for retirement while allowing the savings to grow tax free. Taxes are paid on contributions, but withdrawals, subject to certain rules, are not taxed at all.

S

Second Mortgage—A secondary loan obtained on a piece of property. The loan is in second position behind the first mortgage.

Secondary Market—The buying and selling of existing mortgages as part of a "pool" of mortgages or mortgage-backed securities.

Secured Loan—A loan where the borrower pledges some asset as collateral for the loan.

Securities and Exchange Commission (SEC)—A United States government agency that oversees the issuing and exchanging of public securities.

Settlement Statement—Also known as an HUD-1 or closing statement. An itemized list of costs paid at closing for a real estate transaction.

Simplified Employee Pension IRA (SEP-IRA)—A tax-deferred retirement plan for small businesses with fewer than 25 employees and the self-employed. Employers may contribute 25% of compensation or $49,000 (2010), whichever is less.

SIMPLE IRA or SIMPLE 401(k)—This type of plan is available to companies with 100 or fewer employees, who offer no other type of retirement plan. It is similar to a 401(k) plan and offers pretax savings for employees of the company.

Solo 401(k)—Also known as an "individual K." A 401(k) plan combined with a profit-sharing plan available to businesses that have no other employees beyond an owner and a spouse. This plan allows an individual to contribute more than a SEP-IRA or pension plan.

Spousal IRA—An IRA that is established for a nonworking spouse who doesn't receive sufficient compensation to qualify for an IRA. The couple must file a joint tax return.

Subordinate Loan—A loan that is in junior position behind a first mortgage. A second or third mortgage obtained for the same property.

Survey–A precise measurement of a piece of property by a licensed surveyor.

Sweat Equity—Contribution to the improvement of a property in the form of labor or services rather than cash.

T

Tax- and Penalty-free Withdrawals—Qualified transactions that remove money from an IRA without incurring taxes or fines.

Tax Lien—A lien that is placed against a property if the owner hasn't paid their taxes.

Tax-deferred Investment Growth (Traditional IRA)—An IRA whose earnings are not taxable until they begin to be withdrawn from the IRA account.

Tax-free Investment Growth (Roth IRA)—An IRA whose earnings are never taxed, even when distributed from the IRA.

Tenancy in Common—A type of ownership held by two or more owners who have an undivided interest in a property, but not necessarily equally.

Title—The legal document which outlines ownership of the property and other details.

Title Company—A firm that ensures that the property title is clear and provides title insurance. They also oversee the closings of real estate in some states.

Townhouse—An attached home that is not a condominium.

Traditional IRA—Also known as regular IRAs. This type of IRA is tax deferred and not a ROTH, SEP, or SIMPLE IRA.

Transfer—The direct *movement* of assets in an individual retirement account from one custodian/administrator to another. This is not considered a distribution.

Triple Net Lease (NNN)—A lease agreement which requires the tenant to pay all operating costs of the building along with the rent.

Trustee—The individual, bank, or trust company having fiduciary responsibility for holding plan assets.

U

Underwriter—A person who reviews and evaluates an application for a loan.

Underwriting—Analysis of risk and setting of an appropriate rate and term for a mortgage on a given property for specific borrowers.

Unencumbered—A property free of any liens, covenants, or restrictions.

Unrelated Business Taxable Income—Also known as UBIT. Income earned by a tax-exempt entity such as an IRA that does not result from tax-exempt activities. The entity may owe taxes on this income.

Unrelated Debt-Financed Income—Also known as UDFI. Income taxable to an IRA which is attributable to borrowing funds. This applies to income earned from real estate purchased with non-recourse financing. Unrelated debt-financed income is a form of unrelated business taxable income.

RESOURCES

Self-Directed IRA Custodians (alphabetical order)

Equity Trust Company
225 Burns Rd.
Elyria, OH 44035
Toll free: 1-888-382-4727
www.trustetc.com

IRA Services Trust Company
1160 Industrial Rd, Suite 1
San Carlos, CA 94070
Phone: 1-650-593-2221
www.iraservices.com

Lincoln Trust Company
(formerly Fiserv ISS)
717 17th Street, Suite 2200
Denver, CO 80202
Toll free: 1-800-525-2124
www.lincolntrustco.com

Millennium Trust Company, LLC
820 Jorie Boulevard, Suite 420
Oak Brook, IL 60523
Toll free: 1-800-258-7878
www.mtrustcompany.com

PENSCO Trust Company
450 Sansome St., 14th floor
San Francisco, CA 94111
Toll Free: 1-866-818-4472
www.penscotrust.com

Provident Trust Group
8880 W. Sunset Rd., Suite 250
Las Vegas, NV 89148
Toll Free: 1-888-855-9856
www.providentira.com

Self Directed IRA Services, Inc.
600 Congress Ave., Suite 400
Austin, TX 78701
Toll Free: 1-866-928-9394
www.sdiraservices.com

Sterling Trust Company
7901 Fish Pond Road
Waco, TX 76710
Toll Free: 1-800-955-3434
www.sterling-trust.com

Sunwest Trust, Inc.
3240 D Juan Tabo NE
Albuquerque., NM 87111
Toll Free: 1-800-642-7167
www.sunwesttrust.com

Self-Directed IRA Administrators (alphabetical order)

American Pension Services
4168 West 12600 South
Riverton, UT 84096
Phone: 1-801-571-0667
www.aps-utah.com

Capital Real Estate IRA
3 East Stow Road
Marlton, New Jersey 08053
Toll Free: 1-888-996-9899
www.capitalira.com

The Entrust Group
Corporate Headquarters
9444 Double R Boulevard
Suite A
Reno, Nevada 89521
Toll Free: 1-888-340-8977
www.theentrustgroup.com

MyRA Services
518 South 12th Street
Murray, KY 42071
Toll Free: 1-888-753-6972
www.getmyra.com

Polycomp Trust Company
3000 Lava Ridge Court
Suite 130
Roseville, CA 95661
Toll free: 1-800-952-8800
www.polycomp.net

Security Trust Company
223 N. Prospect St, Suite 202
Hagerstown, MD 21740
Toll free: 1-866-682-3683
www.securitytrustcompany.com

Sovereign International Pension Services
1312 Alt 19
Palm Harbor, FL 34683
Phone: 1-727-784-4841
www.sovereignpensionservices.com

**IRA LLC Facilitators
(alphabetical order)**

Asset Exchange Strategies, LLC
2407 S Bagdad Rd
Leander, TX 78641
Toll Free: 1-877-812-4015
www.myrealestateira.com

Guidant Financial Services
13122 NE 20th Street
Suite 100
Bellevue, WA 98005
Toll Free: 1-888-472-4455
www.guidantfinancial.com

IRA Advantage
10220 SW Greenburg Rd, Suite 111
Portland, OR 97223
Toll Free: 1-800-475-1031
www.iraadvantage.net

IRA Source, LLC
100 Oceangate St., 12th Floor
Long Beach, CA 90802
Phone: 1-562-546-4826
www.irafinancialservices.com

IRAvest, Inc.
2995 Woodside Road, #400
Woodside, CA 94062
Phone: 1-415-816-0056
www.iravest.com

KKO Lawyers
Corporate Office
856 South Sage Drive, Suite 300
Cedar City, Utah 84720
Toll Free: 1-888-801-0010
www.kkolawyers.com

Nabers Group
621 17th St, #2100
Denver, CO 80293
Toll Free: 1-877-903-2220
www.nabers.com

Newman Asset Management, LLC
2950 North Loop West, Suite 500
Houston, TX 77092
Toll Free: 1-888-254-0609
www.newmanassets.com

Safeguard Financial
5800 SW Meadows Road, Suite 240
Lake Oswego, OR 97035
Toll Free: 1-877-229-9763
www.ira123.com

Sage Harbor IRA Investments
555 Second St., Suite 3
Encinitas, CA 92024
Toll Free: 1-877-380-1828
www.sageharbor-ira.com

Self-Directed Retirement Solutions, LLC
5088 Hillsdale Circle
El Dorado Hills, CA 95762
Toll Free: 1-888-878-3472
www.thetrueira.com

Your Entity Solution, LLC
6628 Sky Pointe Drive, Suite 129
Las Vegas, Nevada 89131
Phone: 1-702-506-0190
www.yourentitysolution.com

Solo 401k Facilitators
(alphabetical order)

Nabers Group
621 17th St, #2100
Denver, CO 80293
Toll Free: 1-877-903-2220
www.nabers.com

Safeguard Financial
5800 SW Meadows Road, Suite 240
Lake Oswego, OR 97035
Toll Free: 1-877-229-9763
www.ira123.com

Self-Directed Retirement Solutions, LLC
5088 Hillsdale Circle
El Dorado Hills, CA 95762
Toll Free: 1-888-878-3472
www.thetrueira.com

Self-Directed IRA Associations

Retirement Industry Trust Association
Contact Person:
Mary Mohr
Executive Director
Phone: 1-941-724-0900
www.ritaus.org

Self-Directed IRA Non-Recourse Lender

North American Savings Bank
10950 El Monte, ste 210
Overland Park, KS 66211
Toll Free: 1-866-735-6272
www.iralending.com
www.nasb.com

ADDITIONAL RESOURCES

Internal Revenue Service Publications –

The Internal Revenue Service provides useful and informative tax guidance for consumers in the form of IRS Publications. These publications cover a variety of topics and can be found at www.irs.gov/pub. Publications that include information relevant to Individual Retirement Accounts include:

Publication 590 – Individual Retirement Arrangements (IRAs)
(A condensed version of Publication 590 is located on pages 185-189)

Publication 598 – Tax on Unrelated Business Income of Exempt Organizations (UBIT)

Internal Revenue Code –

The Constitution of the United States empowers Congress to make laws relating to many types of taxes, including income, estate, gift, excise and employment taxes. All tax statutes are published in their entirety as Public Laws and then codified at Title 26 of the United States Code (Title 26 is also known as "the Internal Revenue Code.")

Cornell University Law School provides a free, web-based service to view the Internal Revenue Code. This information can be found at www.law.cornell.edu/uscode.

The code sections most relevant to Individual Retirement Accounts and investing therein include:

Section 408. Individual Retirement Accounts

Section 408A. Roth IRAs

Section 4975. Tax on Prohibited Transactions
(The full length version of Section 4975 is located on pages 191-220)

IRS PUBLICATION 590

**Prohibited Transactions and Disqualified Individuals (condensed version).
The entire version can be found at www.irs.gov/pub/irs-pdf/p590.pdf**

Generally, a prohibited transaction is any improper use of your traditional IRA account or annuity by you, your beneficiary, or any disqualified person. Disqualified persons include your fiduciary and members of your family (spouse, ancestor, lineal descendant, and any spouse of a lineal descendant).

The following are examples of prohibited transactions with a traditional IRA.

- **Borrowing money from it.**

- **Selling property to it.**

- **Receiving unreasonable compensation for managing it.**

- **Using it as security for a loan.**

- **Buying property for personal use (present or future) with IRA funds.**

Fiduciary. For these purposes, a fiduciary includes anyone who does any of the following.

- **Exercises any discretionary authority or discretionary control in managing your IRA or exercises any authority or control in managing or disposing of its assets.**

- **Provides investment advice to your IRA for a fee, or has any authority or responsibility to do so.**

- **Has any discretionary authority or discretionary responsibility in administering your IRA.**

Effect on an IRA account. Generally, if you or your beneficiary engages in a prohibited transaction in connection with your traditional IRA account at any time during the year, the account stops being an IRA as of the first day of that year.

Effect on you or your beneficiary. If your account stops being an IRA because you or your beneficiary engaged in a prohibited transaction, the account is treated as distributing all its assets to you at their fair market values on the first day of the year. If the total of those values is more than your basis in the IRA, you will have a taxable gain that is includible in your income. For information on figuring your gain and reporting it in income, see Are Distributions Taxable, earlier. The distribution may be subject to additional taxes or penalties.

Borrowing on an annuity contract. If you borrow money against your traditional IRA annuity contract, you must include in your gross income the fair market value of the annuity contract as of the first day of your tax year. You may have to pay the 10% additional tax on early distributions, discussed later.

Pledging an account as security. If you use a part of your traditional IRA account as security for a loan, that part is treated as a distribution and is included in your gross income. You may have to pay the 10% additional tax on early distributions, discussed later.

Trust account set up by an employer or an employee association. Your account or annuity does not lose its IRA treatment if your employer or the employee association with whom you have your traditional IRA engages in a prohibited transaction.

Owner participation. If you participate in the prohibited transaction with your employer or the association, your account is no longer treated as an IRA.

Taxes on prohibited transactions. If someone other than the owner or beneficiary of a traditional IRA engages in a prohibited transaction, that person may be liable for certain taxes. In general, there is a 15% tax on the amount of the prohibited transaction and a 100% additional tax if the transaction is not corrected.

Loss of IRA status. If the traditional IRA ceases to be an IRA because of a prohibited transaction by you or your beneficiary, you or your beneficiary are not liable for these excise taxes. However, you or your beneficiary may have to pay other taxes as discussed under Effect on you or your beneficiary, earlier.

Exempt Transactions

The following two types of transactions are not prohibited transactions if they meet the requirements that follow.

- **Payments of cash, property, or other consideration by the sponsor of your traditional IRA to you (or members of your family).**

- **Your receipt of services at reduced or no cost from the bank where your traditional IRA is established or maintained.**

Payments of cash, property, or other consideration. Even if a sponsor makes payments to you or your family, there is no prohibited transaction if all three of the following requirements are met.

1. **The payments are for establishing a traditional IRA or for making additional contributions to it.**

2. **The IRA is established solely to benefit you, your spouse, and your or your spouse's beneficiaries.**

3. **During the year, the total fair market value of the payments you receive is not more than:**

a. **$10 for IRA deposits of less than $5,000, or**

b. $20 for IRA deposits of $5,000 or more.

If the consideration is group term life insurance, requirements (1) and (3) do not apply if no more than $5,000 of the face value of the insurance is based on a dollar- for-dollar basis on the assets in your IRA.

Services received at reduced or no cost. Even if a sponsor provides services at reduced or no cost, there is no prohibited transaction if all of the following requirements are met.

- The traditional IRA qualifying you to receive the services is established and maintained for the benefit of you, your spouse, and your or your spouse's beneficiaries.

- The bank itself can legally offer the services.

- The services are provided in the ordinary course of business by the bank (or a bank affiliate) to customers who qualify but do not maintain an IRA (or a Keogh plan).

- The determination, for a traditional IRA, of who qualifies for these services is based on an IRA (or a Keogh plan) deposit balance equal to the lowest qualifying balance for any other type of account.

- The rate of return on a traditional IRA investment that qualifies is not less than the return on an identical investment that could have been made at the same time at the same branch of the bank by a customer who is not eligible for (or does not receive) these services.

Investment in Collectibles

If your traditional IRA invests in collectibles, the amount invested is considered distributed to you in the year invested. You may have to pay the 10% additional tax on early distributions, discussed later.

- Collectibles. These include:

- Artworks,

- Rugs,

- **Antiques,**

- **Metals,**

- **Gems,**

- **Stamps,**

- **Coins,**

- **Alcoholic beverages, and**

- **Certain other tangible personal property.**

Exception. Your IRA can invest in one, one-half, one-quarter, or one-tenth ounce U.S. gold coins, or one-ounce silver coins minted by the Treasury Department. It can also invest in certain platinum coins and certain gold, silver, palladium, and platinum bullion.

INTERNAL REVENUE CODE SECTION 4975

Tax on Prohibited Transactions and Disqualified Individuals

(a) Initial taxes on disqualified person

There is hereby imposed a tax on each prohibited transaction. The rate of tax shall be equal to 15 percent of the amount involved with respect to the prohibited transaction for each year (or part thereof) in the taxable period. The tax imposed by this subsection shall be paid by any disqualified person who participates in the prohibited transaction (other than a fiduciary acting only as such).

(b) Additional taxes on disqualified person

In any case in which an initial tax is imposed by subsection (a) on a prohibited transaction and the transaction is not corrected within the taxable period, there is hereby imposed a tax equal to 100 percent of the amount involved. The tax imposed by this subsection shall be paid by any disqualified person who participated in the prohibited transaction (other than a fiduciary acting only as such).

(c) Prohibited transaction

(1) General rule

For purposes of this section, the term "prohibited transaction" means any direct or indirect—

(A) sale or exchange, or leasing, of any property between a plan and a disqualified person;

(B) lending of money or other extension of credit between a plan and a disqualified person;

(C) furnishing of goods, services, or facilities between a plan and a disqualified person;

(D) transfer to, or use by or for the benefit of, a disqualified person of the income or assets of a plan;

(E) act by a disqualified person who is a fiduciary whereby he deals with the income or assets of a plan in his own interests or for his own account; or

(F) receipt of any consideration for his own personal account by any disqualified person who is a fiduciary from any party dealing with the plan in connection with a transaction involving the income or assets of the plan.

(2) Special exemption

The Secretary shall establish an exemption procedure for purposes of this subsection. Pursuant to such procedure, he may grant a conditional or unconditional exemption of any disqualified person or transaction, orders of disqualified persons or transactions, from all or part of the restrictions imposed by paragraph (1) of this subsection. Action under this subparagraph may be taken only after consultation and coordination with the Secretary of Labor. The Secretary may not grant an exemption under this paragraph unless he finds that such exemption is—

(A) administratively feasible,

(B) in the interests of the plan and of its participants and beneficiaries, and

(C) protective of the rights of participants and beneficiaries of the plan.

Before granting an exemption under this paragraph, the Secretary shall require adequate notice to be given to interested persons and shall publish notice in the Federal Register of the pendency of such exemption and shall afford interested persons an opportunity to present views. No exemption may be granted under this paragraph with respect to a transaction described in subparagraph (E) or (F) of paragraph (1) unless the Secretary affords an opportunity for a hearing and makes a determination on the record with respect to the findings required under subparagraphs (A), (B), and (C) of this paragraph, except that in lieu of such hearing the Secretary may accept any record made by the Secretary of Labor with respect to an application for exemption under section 408(a) of title I of the Employee Retirement Income Security Act of 1974.

(3) Special rule for individual retirement accounts

An individual for whose benefit an individual retirement account is established and his beneficiaries shall be exempt from the tax imposed by this section with respect to any transaction concerning such account (which would otherwise be taxable under this section) if, with respect to such transaction, the account ceases to be an individual retirement account by reason of the application of section 408 (e)(2)(A) or if section 408 (e) (4) applies to such account.

(4) Special rule for Archer MSAs

An individual for whose benefit an Archer MSA (within the meaning of section 220 (d)) is established shall be exempt from the tax imposed by this section with respect to any transaction concerning such account (which would otherwise be taxable under this section) if section 220 (e)(2) applies to such transaction.

(5) Special rule for Coverdell education savings accounts

An individual for whose benefit a Coverdell education savings account is established and any contributor to such account shall be exempt from the tax imposed by this section with respect to any transaction concerning such account (which would otherwise be taxable under this section) if section 530 (d) applies with respect to such transaction.

(6) Special rule for health savings accounts

An individual for whose benefit a health savings account (within the meaning of section 223 (d)) is established shall be exempt from the tax imposed by this section with respect to any transaction concerning such account (which would otherwise be taxable under this section) if, with respect to such transaction, the account ceases to be a health savings account by reason of the application of section 223 (e)(2) to such account.

(d) Exemptions

Except as provided in subsection (f)(6), the prohibitions provided in subsection (c) shall not apply to—

(1) any loan made by the plan to a disqualified person who is a participant or beneficiary of the plan if such loan—

(A) is available to all such participants or beneficiaries on a reasonably equivalent basis,

(B) is not made available to highly compensated employees (within the meaning of section 414 (q)) in an amount greater than the amount made available to other employees,

(C) is made in accordance with specific provisions regarding such loans set forth in the plan,

(D) bears a reasonable rate of interest, and

(E) is adequately secured;

(2) any contract, or reasonable arrangement, made with a disqualified person for office space, or legal, accounting, or other services necessary for the establishment or operation of the plan, if no more than reasonable compensation is paid therefor;

(3) any loan to an [1] leveraged employee stock ownership plan (as defined in subsection (e)(7)), if—

(A) such loan is primarily for the benefit of participants and beneficiaries of the plan, and

(B) such loan is at a reasonable rate of interest, and any collateral which is given to a disqualified person by the plan consists only of qualifying employer securities (as defined in subsection (e)(8));

(4) the investment of all or part of a plan's assets in deposits which bear a reasonable interest rate in a bank or similar financial institution supervised by the United States or a State, if such bank or other institution is a fiduciary of such plan and if—

(A) the plan covers only employees of such bank or other institution and employees of affiliates of such bank or other institution, or

(B) such investment is expressly authorized by a provision of the plan or by a fiduciary (other than such bank or institution or affiliates thereof) who is expressly empowered by the plan to so instruct the trustee with respect to such investment;

(5) any contract for life insurance, health insurance, or annuities with one or more insurers which are qualified to do business in a State if the plan pays no more than adequate consideration, and if each such insurer or insurers is—

(A) the employer maintaining the plan, or

(B) a disqualified person which is wholly owned (directly or indirectly) by the employer establishing the plan, or by any person which is a disqualified person with respect to the plan, but only if the total premiums and annuity considerations written by such insurers for life insurance, health insurance, or annuities for all plans (and their employers) with respect to which such insurers are disqualified persons (not including premiums or annuity considerations written by the employer maintaining the plan) do not exceed 5 percent of the total premiums and annuity considerations written for all lines of insurance in that year by such insurers (not including premiums or annuity considerations written by the employer maintaining the plan);

(6) the provision of any ancillary service by a bank or similar financial institution supervised by the United States or a State, if such service is provided at not more than reasonable compensation, if such bank or other institution is a fiduciary of such plan, and if—

(A) such bank or similar financial institution has adopted adequate internal safeguards which assure that the provision of such ancillary service is consistent with sound banking and financial practice, as determined by Federal or State supervisory authority, and

(B) the extent to which such ancillary service is provided is subject to specific guidelines issued by such bank or similar financial institution (as determined by the Secretary after consultation with Federal and State supervisory authority), and under such guidelines the bank or similar financial institution does not provide such ancillary service—

(i) in an excessive or unreasonable manner, and

(ii) in a manner that would be inconsistent with the best interests of participants and beneficiaries of employee benefit plans;

(7) the exercise of a privilege to convert securities, to the extent provided in regulations of the Secretary but only if the plan receives no less than adequate consideration pursuant to such conversion;

(8) any transaction between a plan and a common or collective trust fund or pooled investment fund maintained by a disqualified person which is a bank or trust company supervised by a State or Federal agency or between a plan and a pooled investment fund of an insurance company qualified to do business in a State if—

(A) the transaction is a sale or purchase of an interest in the fund,

(B) the bank, trust company, or insurance company receives not more than a reasonable compensation, and

(C) such transaction is expressly permitted by the instrument under which the plan is maintained, or by a fiduciary (other than the bank, trust company, or insurance company, or an affiliate thereof) who has authority to manage and control the assets of the plan;

(9) receipt by a disqualified person of any benefit to which he may be entitled as a participant or beneficiary in the plan, so long as the benefit is computed and paid on a basis which is consistent with the terms of the plan as applied to all other participants and beneficiaries;

(10) receipt by a disqualified person of any reasonable compensation for services rendered, or for the reimbursement of expenses properly and actually incurred, in the performance of his duties with the plan, but no person so serving who already receives full-time pay from an employer or an association of employers, whose employees are participants in the plan or from an employee organization whose members are participants in such plan shall receive compensation from such fund, except for reimbursement of expenses properly and actually incurred;

(11) service by a disqualified person as a fiduciary in addition to being an officer, employee, agent, or other representative of a disqualified person;

(12) the making by a fiduciary of a distribution of the assets of the trust in accordance with the terms of the plan if such assets are distributed in the same manner as provided under section 4044 of title IV of the Employee Retirement Income Security Act of 1974 (relating to allocation of assets);

(13) any transaction which is exempt from section 406 of such Act by reason of section 408(e) of such Act (or which would be so exempt if such section 406 applied to such transaction) or which is exempt from section 406 of such Act by reason of section 408(b)(12) of such Act;

(14) any transaction required or permitted under part 1 of subtitle E of title IV or section 4223 of the Employee Retirement Income Security Act of 1974, but this paragraph shall not apply with respect to the application of subsection (c)(1) (E) or (F);

(15) a merger of multiemployer plans, or the transfer of assets or liabilities between multiemployer plans, determined by the Pension Benefit Guaranty Corporation to meet the requirements of section 4231 of such Act, but this paragraph shall not apply with respect to the application of subsection (c)(1)(E) or (F);

(16) a sale of stock held by a trust which constitutes an individual retirement account under section 408 (a) to the individual for whose benefit such account is established if—

(A) such stock is in a bank (as defined in section 581) or a depository institution holding company (as defined in section 3(w)(1) of the Federal Deposit Insurance Act (12 U.S.C. 1813 (w)(1)),[2]

(B) such stock is held by such trust as of the date of the enactment of this paragraph,

(C) such sale is pursuant to an election under section 1362 (a) by such bank or company,

(D) such sale is for fair market value at the time of sale (as established by an independent appraiser) and the terms of the sale are otherwise at least as favorable to such trust as the terms that would apply on a sale to an unrelated party,

(E) such trust does not pay any commissions, costs, or other expenses in connection with the sale, and

(F) the stock is sold in a single transaction for cash not later than 120 days after the S corporation election is made;

(17) Any [3] transaction in connection with the provision of investment advice described in subsection (e)(3)(B) to a participant or beneficiary in a plan that permits such participant or beneficiary to direct the investment of plan assets in an individual account, if—

(A) the transaction is—

(i) the provision of the investment advice to the participant or beneficiary of the plan with respect to a security or other property available as an investment under the plan,

(ii) the acquisition, holding, or sale of a security or other property available as an investment under the plan pursuant to the investment advice, or

(iii) the direct or indirect receipt of fees or other compensation by the fiduciary adviser or an affiliate thereof (or any employee, agent, or registered representative of the fiduciary adviser or affiliate) in connection with the provision of the advice or in connection with an acquisition, holding, or sale of a security or other property available as an investment under the plan pursuant to the investment advice; and

(B) the requirements of subsection (f)(8) are met,[4]

(18) any transaction involving the purchase or sale of securities, or other property (as determined by the Secretary of Labor), between a plan and a disqualified person (other than a fiduciary described in subsection (e)(3)) with respect to a plan if—

(A) the transaction involves a block trade,

(B) at the time of the transaction, the interest of the plan (together with the interests of any other plans maintained by the same plan sponsor), does not exceed 10 percent of the aggregate size of the block trade,

(C) the terms of the transaction, including the price, are at least as favorable to the plan as an arm's length [5] transaction, and

(D) the compensation associated with the purchase and sale is not greater than the compensation associated with an arm's length [5] transaction with an unrelated party,[4]

(19) any transaction involving the purchase or sale of securities, or other property (as determined by the Secretary of Labor), between a plan and a disqualified person if—

(A) the transaction is executed through an electronic communication network, alternative trading system, or similar execution system or trading venue subject to regulation and oversight by—

(i) the applicable Federal regulating entity, or

(ii) such foreign regulatory entity as the Secretary of Labor may determine by regulation,

(B) either—

(i) the transaction is effected pursuant to rules designed to match purchases and sales at the best price available through the execution system in accordance with applicable rules of the Securities and Exchange Commission or other relevant governmental authority, or

(ii) neither the execution system nor the parties to the transaction take into account the identity of the parties in the execution of trades,

(C) the price and compensation associated with the purchase and sale are not greater than the price and compensation associated with an arm's length [5] transaction with an unrelated party,

(D) if [6] the disqualified person has an ownership interest in the system or venue described in subparagraph (A), the system or venue has been authorized by the plan sponsor or other independent fiduciary for transactions described in this paragraph, and

(E) not less than 30 days prior to the initial transaction described in this paragraph executed through any system or venue described in subparagraph (A), a plan fiduciary is provided written or electronic notice of the execution of such transaction through such system or venue,[4]

(20) transactions described in subparagraphs (A), (B), and (D) of subsection (c)(1) between a plan and a person that is a disqualified person other than a fiduciary (or an affiliate) who has or exercises any discretionary authority or control with respect to the investment of the plan assets involved in the transaction or renders investment advice (within the meaning of subsection (e)(3)(B)) with respect to those assets, solely by reason of providing services to the plan or solely by reason of a relationship to such a service provider described in subparagraph (F), (G), (H), or (I) of subsection (e)(2), or both, but only if in connection with such transaction the plan receives no less, nor pays no more, than adequate consideration,[4]

(21) any foreign exchange transactions, between a bank or broker-dealer (or any affiliate of either) and a plan (as defined in this section) with respect to which such bank or broker-dealer (or affiliate) is a trustee, custodian, fiduciary, or other disqualified person person,[7] if—

(A) the transaction is in connection with the purchase, holding, or sale of securities or other investment assets (other than a foreign exchange transaction unrelated to any other investment in securities or other investment assets),

(B) at the time the foreign exchange transaction is entered into, the terms of the transaction are not less favorable to the plan than the terms generally available in comparable arm's length [5] foreign exchange transactions between unrelated parties, or the terms afforded by the bank or broker-dealer (or any affiliate of either) in comparable arm's-length foreign exchange transactions involving unrelated parties,

(C) the exchange rate used by such bank or broker-dealer (or affiliate) for a particular foreign exchange transaction does not deviate by more than 3 percent from the interbank bid and asked rates for transactions of comparable size and maturity at the time of the transaction as displayed on an independent service that reports rates of exchange in the foreign currency market for such currency, and

(D) the bank or broker-dealer (or any affiliate of either) does not have investment discretion, or provide investment advice, with respect to the transaction,[4]

(22) any transaction described in subsection (c)(1)(A) involving the purchase and sale of a security between a plan and any other account managed by the same investment manager, if—

(A) the transaction is a purchase or sale, for no consideration other than cash payment against prompt delivery of a security for which market quotations are readily available,

(B) the transaction is effected at the independent current market price of the security (within the meaning of section 270.17a—7(b) of title 17, Code of Federal Regulations),

(C) no brokerage commission, fee (except for customary transfer fees, the fact of which is disclosed pursuant to subparagraph (D)), or other remuneration is paid in connection with the transaction,

(D) a fiduciary (other than the investment manager engaging in the cross-trades or any affiliate) for each plan participating in the transaction authorizes in advance of any cross-trades (in a document that is separate from any other written agreement of the parties) the investment manager to engage in cross trades at the investment manager's discretion, after such fiduciary has received disclosure regarding the conditions under which cross trades may take place (but only if such disclosure is separate from any other agreement or disclosure involving the asset management relationship), including the written policies and procedures of the investment manager described in subparagraph (H),

(E) each plan participating in the transaction has assets of at least $100,000,000, except that if the assets of a plan are invested in a master trust containing the assets of plans maintained by employers in the same controlled group (as defined in section 407(d)(7) of the Employee Retirement Income Security Act of 1974), the master trust has assets of at least $100,000,000,

(F) the investment manager provides to the plan fiduciary who authorized cross trading under subparagraph (D) a quarterly report detailing all cross trades executed by the investment manager in which the plan participated during such quarter, including the following information, as applicable:

(i) the identity of each security bought or sold;

(ii) the number of shares or units traded;

(iii) the parties involved in the cross-trade; and

(iv) trade price and the method used to establish the trade price,

(G) the investment manager does not base its fee schedule on the plan's consent to cross trading, and no other service (other than the investment opportunities and cost savings available through a cross trade) is conditioned on the plan's consent to cross trading,

(H) the investment manager has adopted, and cross-trades are effected in accordance with, written cross-trading policies and procedures that are fair and equitable to all accounts participating in the cross-trading program, and that include a description of the manager's pricing policies and procedures, and the manager's policies and procedures for allocating cross trades in an objective manner among accounts participating in the cross-trading program, and

(I) the investment manager has designated an individual responsible for periodically reviewing such purchases and sales to ensure compliance with the written policies and procedures described in subparagraph (H), and following such review, the individual shall issue an annual written report no later than 90 days following the period to which it relates signed under penalty of perjury to the plan fiduciary who authorized cross trading under subparagraph (D) describing the steps performed during the course of the review, the level of compliance, and any specific instances of noncompliance.

The written report shall also notify the plan fiduciary of the plan's right to terminate participation in the investment manager's cross-trading program at any time,[4] or

(23) except as provided in subsection (f)(11), a transaction described in subparagraph (A), (B), (C), or (D) of subsection (c)(1) in connection with the acquisition, holding, or disposition of any security or commodity, if the transaction is corrected before the end of the correction period.

(e) Definitions

(1) Plan

For purposes of this section, the term "plan" means—

(A) a trust described in section 401 (a) which forms a part of a plan, or a plan described in section 403 (a), which trust or plan is exempt from tax under section 501 (a),

(B) an individual retirement account described in section 408 (a),

(C) an individual retirement annuity described in section 408 (b),

(D) an Archer MSA described in section 220 (d),

(E) a health savings account described in section 223 (d),

(F) a Coverdell education savings account described in section 530, or

(G) a trust, plan, account, or annuity which, at any time, has been determined by the Secretary to be described in any preceding subparagraph of this paragraph.

(2) Disqualified person

For purposes of this section, the term "disqualified person" means a person who is—

(A) a fiduciary;

(B) a person providing services to the plan;

(C) an employer any of whose employees are covered by the plan;

(D) an employee organization any of whose members are covered by the plan;

(E) an owner, direct or indirect, of 50 percent or more of—

(i) the combined voting power of all classes of stock entitled to vote or the total value of shares of all classes of stock of a corporation,

(ii) the capital interest or the profits interest of a partnership, or

(iii) the beneficial interest of a trust or unincorporated enterprise,

which is an employer or an employee organization described in subparagraph (C) or (D);

(F) a member of the family (as defined in paragraph (6)) of any individual described in subparagraph (A), (B), (C), or (E);

(G) a corporation, partnership, or trust or estate of which (or in which) 50 percent or more of—

(i) the combined voting power of all classes of stock entitled to vote or the total value of shares of all classes of stock of such corporation,

(ii) the capital interest or profits interest of such partnership, or

(iii) the beneficial interest of such trust or estate,

is owned directly or indirectly, or held by persons described in subparagraph (A), (B), (C), (D), or (E);

(H) an officer, director (or an individual having powers or responsibilities similar to those of officers or directors), a 10 percent or more shareholder, or a highly compensated employee (earning 10 percent or more of the yearly wages of an employer) of a person described in subparagraph (C), (D), (E), or (G); or

(I) a 10 percent or more (in capital or profits) partner or joint venturer of a person described in subparagraph (C), (D), (E), or (G).

The Secretary, after consultation and coordination with the Secretary of Labor or his delegate, may by regulation prescribe a percentage lower than 50 percent for subparagraphs (E) and (G) and lower than 10 percent for subparagraphs (H) and (I).

(3) Fiduciary

For purposes of this section, the term "fiduciary" means any person who—

(A) exercises any discretionary authority or discretionary control respecting management of such plan or exercises any authority or control respecting management or disposition of its assets,

(B) renders investment advice for a fee or other compensation, direct or indirect, with respect to any moneys or other property of such plan, or has any authority or responsibility to do so, or

(C) has any discretionary authority or discretionary responsibility in the administration of such plan.

Such term includes any person designated under section 405(c)(1)(B) of the Employee Retirement Income Security Act of 1974.

(4) Stockholdings

For purposes of paragraphs (2)(E)(i) and (G)(i) there shall be taken into account indirect stockholdings which would be taken into account under section 267 (c), except that, for purposes of this paragraph, section 267 (c)(4) shall be treated as providing that the members of the family of an individual are the members within the meaning of paragraph (6).

(5) Partnerships; trusts

For purposes of paragraphs (2)(E)(ii) and (iii), (G)(ii) and (iii), and (I) the ownership of profits or beneficial interests shall be determined in accordance with the rules for constructive ownership of stock provided in section 267 (c) (other than paragraph (3) thereof), except that section 267 (c)(4) shall be treated as providing that the members of the family of an individual are the members within the meaning of paragraph (6).

(6) Member of family

For purposes of paragraph (2)(F), the family of any individual shall include his spouse, ancestor, lineal descendant, and any spouse of a lineal descendant.

(7) Employee stock ownership plan

The term "employee stock ownership plan" means a defined contribution plan—

(A) which is a stock bonus plan which is qualified, or a stock bonus and a money purchase plan both of which are qualified under section 401 (a), and which are designed to invest primarily in qualifying employer securities; and

(B) which is otherwise defined in regulations prescribed by the Secretary.

A plan shall not be treated as an employee stock ownership plan unless it meets the requirements of section 409 (h), section 409(o), and, if applicable, section 409 (n), section 409(p), and section 664 (g) and, if the employer has a registration-type class of securities (as defined in section 409 (e)(4)), it meets the requirements of section 409 (e).

(8) Qualifying employer security

The term "qualifying employer security" means any employer security within the meaning of section 409 (l). If any moneys or other property of a plan are invested in shares of an investment company registered under the Investment Company Act of 1940, the investment shall not cause that investment company or that investment company's investment adviser or principal underwriter to be treated as a fiduciary or a disqualified person for purposes of this section, except when an investment company or its investment adviser or principal underwriter acts in connection with a plan covering employees of the investment company, its investment adviser, or its principal underwriter.

(9) Section made applicable to withdrawal liability payment funds

For purposes of this section—

(A) In general

The term "plan" includes a trust described in section 501 (c)(22).

(B) Disqualified person

In the case of any trust to which this section applies by reason of subparagraph (A), the term "disqualified person" includes any person who is a disqualified person with respect to any plan to which such trust is permitted to make payments under section 4223 of the Employee Retirement Income Security Act of 1974.

(f) Other definitions and special rules

For purposes of this section—

(1) Joint and several liability

If more than one person is liable under subsection (a) or (b) with respect to any one prohibited transaction, all such persons shall be jointly and severally liable under such subsection with respect to such transaction.

(2) Taxable period

The term "taxable period" means, with respect to any prohibited transaction, the period beginning with the date on which the prohibited transaction occurs and ending on the earliest of—

(A) the date of mailing a notice of deficiency with respect to the tax imposed by subsection (a) under section 6212,

(B) the date on which the tax imposed by subsection (a) is assessed, or

(C) the date on which correction of the prohibited transaction is completed.

(3) Sale or exchange; encumbered property

A transfer or real or personal property by a disqualified person to a plan shall be treated as a sale or exchange if the property is subject to a mortgage or similar lien which the plan assumes or if it is subject to a mortgage or similar lien which a disqualified person placed on the property within the 10-year period ending on the date of the transfer.

(4) Amount involved

The term "amount involved" means, with respect to a prohibited transaction, the greater of the amount of money and the fair market value of the other property given or the amount of money and the fair market value of the other property received; except that, in the case of services described in paragraphs (2) and (10) of subsection (d) the amount involved shall be only the excess compensation. For purposes of the preceding sentence, the fair market value—

(A) in the case of the tax imposed by subsection (a), shall be determined as of the date on which the prohibited transaction occurs; and

(B) in the case of the tax imposed by subsection (b), shall be the highest fair market value during the taxable period.

(5) Correction

The terms "correction" and "correct" mean, with respect to a prohibited transaction, undoing the transaction to the extent possible, but in any case placing the plan in a financial position not worse than that in which it would be if the disqualified person were acting under the highest fiduciary standards.

(6) Exemptions not to apply to certain transactions

(A) In general

In the case of a trust described in section 401 (a) which is part of a plan providing contributions or benefits for employees some or all of whom are owner-employees (as defined in section 401 (c)(3)), the exemptions provided by subsection (d) (other than paragraphs (9) and (12)) shall not apply to a transaction in which the plan directly or indirectly—

(i) lends any part of the corpus or income of the plan to,

(ii) pays any compensation for personal services rendered to the plan to, or

(iii) acquires for the plan any property from, or sells any property to,

any such owner-employee, a member of the family (as defined in section 267(c)(4)) of any such owner-employee, or any corporation in which any such owner-employee owns, directly or indirectly, 50 percent or more of the total combined voting power of all classes of stock entitled to vote or 50 percent or more of the total value of shares of all classes of stock of the corporation.

(B) Special rules for shareholder-employees, etc.

(i) In general For purposes of subparagraph (A), the following shall be treated as owner-employees:

(I) A shareholder-employee.

(II) A participant or beneficiary of an individual retirement plan (as defined in section 7701 (a)(37)).

(III) An employer or association of employees which establishes such an individual retirement plan under section 408 (c).

(ii) Exception for certain transactions involving shareholder-employees Subparagraph (A)(iii) shall not apply to a transaction which consists of a sale of employer securities to an employee stock ownership plan (as defined in subsection (e)(7)) by a shareholder-employee, a member of the family (as defined in section 267(c)(4)) of such shareholder-employee, or a corporation in which such a shareholder-employee owns stock representing a 50 percent or greater interest described in subparagraph (A).

(iii) Loan exception For purposes of subparagraph (A)(i), the term "owner-employee" shall only include a person described in subclause (II) or (III) of clause (i).

(C) Shareholder-employee

For purposes of subparagraph (B), the term "shareholder-employee" means an employee or officer of an S corporation who owns (or is considered as owning within the meaning of section 318 (a)(1)) more than 5 percent of the outstanding stock of the corporation on any day during the taxable year of such corporation.

(7) S corporation repayment of loans for qualifying employer securities

A plan shall not be treated as violating the requirements of section 401 or 409 or subsection (e)(7), or as engaging in a prohibited transaction for purposes of subsection (d)(3), merely by reason of any distribution (as described in section 1368 (a)) with respect to S corporation stock that constitutes qualifying employer securities, which in accordance with the plan provisions is used to make payments on a loan described in subsection (d)(3) the proceeds of which were used to acquire such qualifying employer securities (whether or not allocated to participants). The preceding sentence shall not apply in the case of a distribution which is paid with respect to any employer security which is allocated to a participant unless the plan provides that employer securities with a fair market value of not less than the amount of such distribution are allocated to such participant for the year which (but for the preceding sentence) such distribution would have been allocated to such participant.

(8) Provision of investment advice to participant and beneficiaries

(A) In general

The prohibitions provided in subsection (c) shall not apply to transactions described in subsection (d)(17) if the investment advice provided by a fiduciary adviser is provided under an eligible investment advice arrangement.

(B) Eligible investment advice arrangement

For purposes of this paragraph, the term "eligible investment advice arrangement" means an arrangement—

(i) which either—

(I) provides that any fees (including any commission or other compensation) received by the fiduciary adviser for investment advice or with respect to the sale, holding, or acquisition of any security or other property for purposes of investment of plan assets do not vary depending on the basis of any investment option selected, or

(II) uses a computer model under an investment advice program meeting the requirements of subparagraph (C) in connection with the provision of investment advice by a fiduciary adviser to a participant or beneficiary, and

(ii) with respect to which the requirements of subparagraphs (D), (E), (F), (G), (H), and (I) are met.

(C) Investment advice program using computer model

(i) In general An investment advice program meets the requirements of this subparagraph if the requirements of clauses (ii), (iii), and (iv) are met.

(ii) Computer model The requirements of this clause are met if the investment advice provided under the investment advice program is provided pursuant to a computer model that—

(I) applies generally accepted investment theories that take into account the historic returns of different asset classes over defined periods of time,

(II) utilizes relevant information about the participant, which may include age, life expectancy, retirement age, risk tolerance, other assets or sources of income, and preferences as to certain types of investments,

(III) utilizes prescribed objective criteria to provide asset allocation portfolios comprised of investment options available under the plan,

(IV) operates in a manner that is not biased in favor of investments offered by the fiduciary adviser or a person with a material affiliation or contractual relationship with the fiduciary adviser, and

(V) takes into account all investment options under the plan in specifying how a participant's account balance should be invested and is not inappropriately weighted with respect to any investment option.

(iii) Certification

(I) In general The requirements of this clause are met with respect to any investment advice program if an eligible investment expert certifies, prior to the utilization of the computer model and in accordance with rules prescribed by the Secretary of Labor, that the computer model meets the requirements of clause (ii).

(II) Renewal of certifications If, as determined under regulations prescribed by the Secretary of Labor, there are material modifications to a computer model, the requirements of this clause are met only if a certification described in subclause (I) is obtained with respect to the computer model as so modified.

(III) Eligible investment expert The term "eligible investment expert" means any person which meets such requirements as the Secretary of Labor may provide and which does not bear any material affiliation or contractual relationship with any investment adviser or a related person thereof (or any employee, agent, or registered representative of the investment adviser or related person).

(iv) Exclusivity of recommendation The requirements of this clause are met with respect to any investment advice program if—

(I) the only investment advice provided under the program is the advice generated by the computer model described in clause (ii), and

(II) any transaction described in (d)(17)(A)(ii) [8] occurs solely at the direction of the participant or beneficiary.

Nothing in the preceding sentence shall preclude the participant or beneficiary from requesting investment advice other than that described in clause (i), but only if such request has not been solicited by any person connected with carrying out the arrangement.

(D) Express authorization by separate fiduciary

The requirements of this subparagraph are met with respect to an arrangement if the arrangement is expressly authorized by a plan fiduciary other than the person offering the investment advice program, any person providing investment options under the plan, or any affiliate of either.

(E) Audits

(i) In general The requirements of this subparagraph are met if an independent auditor, who has appropriate technical training or experience and proficiency and so represents in writing—

(I) conducts an annual audit of the arrangement for compliance with the requirements of this paragraph, and

(II) following completion of the annual audit, issues a written report to the fiduciary who authorized use of the arrangement which presents its specific findings regarding compliance of the arrangement with the requirements of this paragraph.

(ii) Special rule for individual retirement and similar plans In the case of a plan described in subparagraphs (B) through (F) (and so much of subparagraph (G) as relates to such subparagraphs) of subsection (e)(1), in lieu of the requirements of clause (i), audits of the arrangement shall be conducted at such times and in such manner as the Secretary of Labor may prescribe.

(iii) Independent auditor For purposes of this subparagraph, an auditor is considered independent if it is not related to the person offering the arrangement to the plan and is not related to any person providing investment options under the plan.

(F) Disclosure

The requirements of this subparagraph are met if—

(i) the fiduciary adviser provides to a participant or a beneficiary before the initial provision of the investment advice with regard to any security or other property offered as an investment option, a written notification (which may consist of notification by means of electronic communication)—

(I) of the role of any party that has a material affiliation or contractual relationship with the fiduciary adviser,[9] in the development of the investment advice program and in the selection of investment options available under the plan,

(II) of the past performance and historical rates of return of the investment options available under the plan,

(III) of all fees or other compensation relating to the advice that the fiduciary adviser or any affiliate thereof is to receive (including compensation provided by any third party) in connection with the provision of the advice or in connection with the sale, acquisition, or holding of the security or other property,

(IV) of any material affiliation or contractual relationship of the fiduciary adviser or affiliates thereof in the security or other property,

(V) the [10] manner, and under what circumstances, any participant or beneficiary information provided under the arrangement will be used or disclosed,

(VI) of the types of services provided by the fiduciary adviser in connection with the provision of investment advice by the fiduciary adviser,

(VII) that the adviser is acting as a fiduciary of the plan in connection with the provision of the advice, and

(VIII) that a recipient of the advice may separately arrange for the provision of advice by another adviser, that could have no material affiliation with and receive no fees or other compensation in connection with the security or other property, and

(ii) at all times during the provision of advisory services to the participant or beneficiary, the fiduciary adviser—

(I) maintains the information described in clause (i) in accurate form and in the manner described in subparagraph (H),

(II) provides, without charge, accurate information to the recipient of the advice no less frequently than annually,

(III) provides, without charge, accurate information to the recipient of the advice upon request of the recipient, and

(IV) provides, without charge, accurate information to the recipient of the advice concerning any material change to the information required to be provided to the recipient of the advice at a time reasonably contemporaneous to the change in information.

(G) Other conditions

The requirements of this subparagraph are met if—

(i) the fiduciary adviser provides appropriate disclosure, in connection with the sale, acquisition, or holding of the security or other property, in accordance with all applicable securities laws,

(ii) the sale, acquisition, or holding occurs solely at the direction of the recipient of the advice,

(iii) the compensation received by the fiduciary adviser and affiliates thereof in connection with the sale, acquisition, or holding of the security or other property is reasonable, and

(iv) the terms of the sale, acquisition, or holding of the security or other property are at least as favorable to the plan as an arm's length [5] transaction would be.

(H) Standards for presentation of information

(i) In general The requirements of this subparagraph are met if the notification required to be provided to participants and beneficiaries under subparagraph (F)(i) is written in a clear and conspicuous manner and in a manner calculated to be understood by the average plan participant and is sufficiently accurate and comprehensive to reasonably apprise such participants and beneficiaries of the information required to be provided in the notification.

(ii) Model form for disclosure of fees and other compensation The Secretary of Labor shall issue a model form for the disclosure of fees and other compensation required in subparagraph (F)(i)(III) which meets the requirements of clause (i).

(I) Maintenance for 6 years of evidence of compliance

The requirements of this subparagraph are met if a fiduciary adviser who has provided advice referred to in subparagraph (A) maintains, for a period of not less than 6 years after the provision of the advice, any records necessary for determining whether the requirements of the preceding provisions of this paragraph and of subsection (d)(17) have been met. A transaction prohibited under subsection (c) shall not be considered to have occurred solely because the records are lost or destroyed prior to the end of the 6-year period due to circumstances beyond the control of the fiduciary adviser.

(J) Definitions

For purposes of this paragraph and subsection (d)(17)—

(i) Fiduciary adviser The term "fiduciary adviser" means, with respect to a plan, a person who is a fiduciary of the plan by reason of the provision of investment advice referred to in subsection (e)(3)(B) by the person to a participant or beneficiary of the plan and who is—

(I) registered as an investment adviser under the Investment Advisers Act of 1940 (15 U.S.C. 80b—1 et seq.) or under the laws of the State in which the fiduciary maintains its principal office and place of business,

(II) a bank or similar financial institution referred to in subsection (d) (4) or a savings association (as defined in section 3(b)(1) of the Federal Deposit Insurance Act (12 U.S.C. 1813 (b)(1)), but only if the advice is provided through a trust department of the bank or similar financial institution or savings association which is subject to periodic examination and review by Federal or State banking authorities,

(III) an insurance company qualified to do business under the laws of a State,

(IV) a person registered as a broker or dealer under the Securities Exchange Act of 1934 (15 U.S.C. 78a et seq.),

(V) an affiliate of a person described in any of subclauses (I) through (IV), or

(VI) an employee, agent, or registered representative of a person described in subclauses (I) through (V) who satisfies the requirements of applicable insurance, banking, and securities laws relating to the provision of the advice.

For purposes of this title, a person who develops the computer model described in subparagraph (C)(ii) or markets the investment advice program or computer model shall be treated as a person who is a fiduciary of the plan by reason of the provision of investment advice referred to in subsection (e)(3)(B) to a participant or beneficiary and shall be treated as a fiduciary adviser for purposes of this paragraph and subsection (d)(17), except that the Secretary of Labor may prescribe rules under which only 1 fiduciary adviser may elect to be treated as a fiduciary with respect to the plan.

(ii) Affiliate The term "affiliate" of another entity means an affiliated person of the entity (as defined in section 2(a)(3) of the Investment Company Act of 1940 (15 U.S.C. 80a—2 (a)(3))).

(iii) Registered representative The term "registered representative" of another entity means a person described in section 3(a)(18) of the Securities Exchange Act of 1934 (15 U.S.C. 78c (a)(18)) (substituting the entity for the broker or dealer referred to in such section) or a person described in section 202(a)(17) of the Investment Advisers Act of 1940 (15 U.S.C. 80b—2 (a)(17)) (substituting the entity for the investment adviser referred to in such section).

(9) Block trade

The term "block trade" means any trade of at least 10,000 shares or with a market value of at least $200,000 which will be allocated across two or more unrelated client accounts of a fiduciary.

(10) Adequate consideration

The term "adequate consideration" means—

(A) in the case of a security for which there is a generally recognized market—

(i) the price of the security prevailing on a national securities exchange which is registered under section 6 of the Securities Exchange Act of

1934, taking into account factors such as the size of the transaction and marketability of the security, or

(ii) if the security is not traded on such a national securities exchange, a price not less favorable to the plan than the offering price for the security as established by the current bid and asked prices quoted by persons independent of the issuer and of the party in interest, taking into account factors such as the size of the transaction and marketability of the security, and

(B) in the case of an asset other than a security for which there is a generally recognized market, the fair market value of the asset as determined in good faith by a fiduciary or fiduciaries in accordance with regulations prescribed by the Secretary of Labor.

(11) Correction period

(A) In general

For purposes of subsection (d)(23), the term "correction period" means the 14-day period beginning on the date on which the disqualified person discovers, or reasonably should have discovered, that the transaction would (without regard to this paragraph and subsection (d)(23)) constitute a prohibited transaction.

(B) Exceptions

(i) Employer securities Subsection (d)(23) does not apply to any transaction between a plan and a plan sponsor or its affiliates that involves the acquisition or sale of an employer security (as defined in section 407(d)(1) of the Employee Retirement Income Security Act of 1974) or the acquisition, sale, or lease of employer real property (as defined in section 407(d)(2) of such Act).

(ii) Knowing prohibited transaction In the case of any disqualified person, subsection (d)(23) does not apply to a transaction if, at the time the transaction is entered into, the disqualified person knew (or reasonably should have known) that the transaction would (without regard to this paragraph) constitute a prohibited transaction.

(C) Abatement of tax where there is a correction

If a transaction is not treated as a prohibited transaction by reason of subsection (d)(23), then no tax under subsections (a) and (b) shall be assessed with respect to such transaction, and if assessed the assessment shall be abated, and if collected shall be credited or refunded as an overpayment.

(D) Definitions

For purposes of this paragraph and subsection (d)(23)—

(i) Security The term "security" has the meaning given such term by section 475 (c)(2) (without regard to subparagraph (F)(iii) and the last sentence thereof).

(ii) Commodity The term "commodity" has the meaning given such term by section 475 (e)(2) (without regard to subparagraph (D)(iii) thereof).

(iii) Correct The term "correct" means, with respect to a transaction—

(I) to undo the transaction to the extent possible and in any case to make good to the plan or affected account any losses resulting from the transaction, and

(II) to restore to the plan or affected account any profits made through the use of assets of the plan.

(g) Application of section

This section shall not apply—

(1) in the case of a plan to which a guaranteed benefit policy (as defined in section 401(b)(2)(B) of the Employee Retirement Income Security Act of 1974) is issued, to any assets of the insurance company, insurance service, or insurance organization merely because of its issuance of such policy;

(2) to a governmental plan (within the meaning of section 414 (d)); or

(3) to a church plan (within the meaning of section 414 (e)) with respect to which the election provided by section 410 (d) has not been made.

In the case of a plan which invests in any security issued by an investment company registered under the Investment Company Act of 1940, the assets of such plan shall be deemed to include such security but shall not, by reason of such investment, be deemed to include any assets of such company.

(h) Notification of Secretary of Labor

Before sending a notice of deficiency with respect to the tax imposed by subsection (a) or (b), the Secretary shall notify the Secretary of Labor and provide him a reasonable opportunity to obtain a correction of the prohibited transaction or to comment on the imposition of such tax.

(i) Cross reference

For provisions concerning coordination procedures between Secretary of Labor and Secretary of the Treasury with respect to application of tax imposed by this section and for authority to waive imposition of the tax imposed by subsection (b), see section 3003 of the Employee Retirement Income Security Act of 1974.

INDEX